Volunteering in
New York City

7/26/98

This Book belongs
to Anna Statt
743-1782

Volunteering in New York City

YOUR GUIDE TO WORKING SMALL MIRACLES IN THE BIG APPLE

Richard Mintzer

Walker and Company
New York

First published in the United States of America in 1996 by Walker
Publishing Company, Inc.

Published simultaneously in Canada by Thomas Allen & Son Canada,
Limited, Markham, Ontario

Library of Congress Cataloging-in-Publication Data
Mintzer, Richard.
Volunteering in New York City: your guide to working small
miracles in the Big Apple/Richard Mintzer.
p.   cm.
Includes index.
ISBN 0-8027-7481-4 (pbk.)
1.   Voluntarism—New York (N.Y.)—Directories.   2.   Community
development—New York (N.Y.)—Directories.   I.   Title.
HN49.V64M56   1996
302'.14—dc20   95-43161
CIP

Book design by Chris Welch

Printed in the United States of America

2   4   6   8   10   9   7   5   3   1

Contents

Acknowledgments

Volunteering isn't new to me or to my family. My parents, and my sister Kathi, are very active in the Kidney Foundation of New York and my wife and I are active in the Adoptive Parents Committee, a membership adoption support group of a mere 3,000 families in New York. There's something special about volunteering; it's a feeling of being involved. Once you're doing it, you don't question how you make the time or find the energy around work and raising a family . . . you just do. You also make friends and start relationships with all sorts of interesting people.

I'd like to thank Elyse Weisberg, who made this book a reality; I hope she likes the way it turned out. I also want to thank a wonderful editor Liza Miller; Ellen Block, Barbara Abis, and all the people interviewed; in particular, I'd like to thank the United Way and the Yorkville Civic Council for all their help.

I'd like to dedicate this book to my folks and my family plus Felix, Susan, Avery, Elaine, Sam, Barbara, Alan, Clarice, Gerry, Kathy, Sandi, Richard, Arnie, Nina, Christine, Steve, and the many marvelous people who make APC a top-notch volunteer organization. You exemplify what this book is all about: doing for others; concern for children and for the future.

Introduction

Why Volunteer?

Approximately 1.5 million New Yorkers do some kind of volunteer work as part of their monthly, weekly, or even daily routine. Why? Because it presents an opportunity to do something meaningful, something that touches the lives of others in a very human way. Volunteering is also an opportunity to do something special for yourself.

Doing for others: that's the easy part—it means anything from ladling soup to coaching basketball to keeping an HIV/AIDS patient company. Doing for yourself, however—that's the intriguing part. Many people don't realize that volunteering is also a self-fulfilling experience. It's something special that takes you to a place away from work, away from personal pressures. Yes, it's rewarding to help others, but volunteering also offers you an opportunity to exercise skills and abilities that you may not otherwise have the chance to use. Volunteering allows you to communicate with other people in ways that aren't part of your office or home life. Besides this human gratification, volunteering also affords you the opportunity to do a job and do it well without being distracted by office politics or personal relationships.

Other Reasons for Volunteering

Many people volunteer in fields that they might like to pursue as careers or second careers. It's a marvelous way to gain some practical experience in a new field.

Volunteering is also a way to hone your skills or practice your hobby. A writer drafting brochures and press releases for a nonprofit organization is improving his business writing. A singer performing in a hospital ward is tuning up her voice before an audience. One CPA, who loves entertaining children, practices his hobby by playing a clown in hospital wards—to very appreciative audiences.

And there's the satisfaction of giving something back. Volunteers often appreciate what's been done for someone they love or loved. Or, on the flip side, you may be inspired to volunteer in hopes of improving anything from your own neighborhood, to hospital conditions, to the state's foster care system.

Finally there's the sense of responsibility you may have as a member of the human race. Some people can no longer walk by the homeless without wanting to help them. Many want to contribute to the easing of the HIV/AIDS crisis, while others want to do something to help preserve the arts.

Reasons for volunteering are plentiful—and this book can help you find the best way for you to make a difference.

Where to Volunteer

There are over 15,000 volunteer opportunities in the New York City area. Whew! How many people are stuck in "dead-end" volunteer positions they don't like? Very few. Volunteering gives you the opportunity to do something you *do* like.

Below is a list of factors you might use to help you decide on the post that's best for you.

▼ *Interest.* If it's not something you want to do, it's not for you. Volunteering is not supposed to be bad medicine.

▼ *Time commitment.* If you can only give three hours a week, don't sign up for a position asking for at least five. Make a time commitment that's feasible for both you and the people with whom you'll be working.

▼ *Location.* You may be commuting to work every day, so why commute to volunteer? Pick a location that's easily accessible to your home or office. Or visit a part of the city that specifically interests you.

▼ *Learning.* Want to learn a new skill? Here's your chance. If you want to learn data entry, volunteer to work in the office of an organization using computers.

▼ *People.* Make friends; meet people from various cultures and other countries, or people with similar interests. These are all part of the social reasons for volunteering. You might also find it very rewarding to volunteer with a friend, colleague, or family member.

First Impressions

"I never expected there to be so many sick people," complained one volunteer after his first and last day at a hospital.

Your first impression is a significant one; you want to feel that a volunteer position is right for you.

Elyse Weisberg of the Mayor's Voluntary Action Center explains it very simply: "You should get the warm fuzzies. If the atmosphere doesn't strike you right or you don't feel comfortable, it may not be a good place for you and you're not going to want to keep coming back. If they make you feel welcome and comfortable—if you have a sense of purpose—that's what gives you a good feeling."

Of course that sense of belonging doesn't always click on the first visit. Sometimes you need to give the place a chance.

Expectations

It's natural to have high expectations when you sign up to volunteer. People often think they can make a world of difference, and they get discouraged when they don't see earth-shaking results. However, says Elyse Weisberg, "we can only change a little piece of the world at a time." Focus on the ways in which you *do* make a difference.

Scheduling

Many organizations ask volunteers to make a time commitment, be it one, two, or five hours a week or a certain amount of time in a year. Other places call volunteers only when they're needed, and umbrella groups such as New York Cares offer many one-time opportunities for those not looking to make a set commitment.

Those who find the time aren't always sure how they do it, but somehow they just do. In a city the size and scope of New York, you can volunteer at any given time of the day or night and as often as you choose. Some full-timers can volunteer in the mornings or on their way home from the office. To make scheduling easier, they volunteer at a place near work. It's not uncommon to hear about someone volunteering on his or her lunch hour. And there are also weekends.

The Process

You should pursue volunteer opportunities the same way you go about looking for a job. Good working conditions, a comfortable atmosphere, room for advancement, the chance to contribute, and good people to work with are all important factors.

Use the interview process as a chance to ask the interviewer a few questions. Or, if you prefer doing research on your own, a phone call will usually net you a package of volunteering information, including an application to fill out before your interview(s). Your application should convey basic information about you, as well as highlight your likes and dislikes. With luck a perfect match can be found between your interests and the organization's needs—but, as in job hunting, the right place may not be the first one at which you interview.

Requirements

Along with your initial application, you may have to supply references, sometimes personal and sometimes medical. New York State mandates that all hospital volunteers have a PPD test for tuberculosis. Other medical tests are necessary for some opportunities, and if you are applying to work with children, you may be fingerprinted as part of the state-mandated procedure for screening out child abusers.

As for orientation and training, they vary tremendously. Orientation will familiarize you with the organization, its procedures, and its way of meeting various needs and emergencies. Training can take anywhere from 15 minutes to 15 weeks, depending on the facility and the task at hand.

Although all of the above may seem a bit intimidating, it is important for the institutions to know who is representing them, and important for clients, patients, or visitors that you be well trained in your volunteer activity of choice. And once you've passed through the training or orientation you'll experience a sense of belonging.

Associations, Clubs, and Committees

Although we haven't focused on it in our listings, another great way to volunteer is through membership groups. From the local PTA to support groups to work-related organizations, membership in associations and committees is a terrific way to volunteer for a cause that's close to your heart. My own personal experience is that of becoming very active in the Adoptive Parents Committee. My wife and I, in great appreciation of what the support group did to assist and encourage us through the adoption process, both became active volunteers.

Volunteering as a Family

Combining "family time" and "volunteering time" is a wonderful way to grow closer. "We've got to teach kids by example about priorities and values," says Elyse Weisberg. "Family volunteering gives kids a chance to spend time with their parents during which Mom and Dad are not the authoritarian figures. It also gives children a sense of self-worth, as family members see them in a new light."

Many places have teen programs, while others accept 10-, 11-, or 12-year-olds to work with younger children. From planting to cleaning up a park to helping feed the homeless, families can find opportunities to share volunteer work. Consider the option and ask the volunteer coordinators.

About This Book

This book is designed to provide you with a host of opportunities in each of several areas of interest. The listings cover the arts, education, health, community, and more. Naturally there is some overlap, and a few organizations are listed in more than one chapter. Others could easily be listed in three or four different areas, but we chose just one category. So, if you don't see what you're looking for in one section, try another, or look in the index.

The listings that follow may prompt ideas of volunteering in one of the many locations not included here. Obviously there are hospitals, nursing homes, churches, synagogues, community centers, et cetera, throughout the city that aren't covered here, and it's very likely that they offer opportunities that are similar to those listed. Use this book as a guide, or as a springboard for your own volunteering ideas. We hope it helps you get involved.

1

Art and Culture

From Lincoln Center to a wide array of museums, New York City's cultural attractions are not only marvelous places to visit but also offer a host of volunteer opportunities. Much to the surprise of some, there are museums and historical societies in all five boroughs, not just in Manhattan.

Most cultural institutions have volunteer programs to fit any schedule. While being a docent (a highly-trained tour guide) generally requires a serious time commitment, most museums and galleries also offer less time-intensive opportunities, including posts at information desks, in gift shops, and in education departments teaching children about exhibits. Although much of the work—especially administrative work —takes place on weekdays, there are weekend and sometimes evening opportunities as well.

Specialty museums can put you in touch with your area of interest, perhaps an area you don't get to focus on in your daily workplace. The Intrepid Museum might have you volunteering on a World War II aircraft carrier, while the Transit Museum might give you a better appreciation for those subways you ride every day.

You might check out local theater groups or dance troupes. If you're looking to get your feet wet in the performing arts you can volunteer to help with set building or costume making. Often community boards (see Community chapter) or neighborhood newspapers will provide you with the best means of finding these more localized operations.

As a volunteer in the arts, you are representing an institution to the public. You may provide a visitor with his or her first, last, or most permanent impression; your answers may fuel discussions, or you may simply point out a rest room to a weary tourist. Either way, you are part of that person's overall experience of the cultural institution—something that gives most volunteers in this arena a great sense of pride.

Why Volunteer at One of the City's Cultural Institutions?

"It's an incredible learning experience" is one frequent answer; "I meet people from all over the world" is another. For some, volunteering is a way to get close to the culture they so admire, while for others it's an opportunity to touch base with their own ethnic heritage. Volunteers often express a good feeling about working in a museum that promotes the history and culture of their own ethnic group.

And then there are the perks. After they've put in some time, volunteers are often privy to certain fringe benefits. Some museum volunteers are granted special privileges in other city cultural institutions as well. There are special exhibitions, lectures, and even classes that you may be able to attend, possibly free of charge.

Tips on Volunteering in the Arts

▼ *Be open to learning, and study your surroundings.* Docent programs and volunteer opportunities in the areas of information and education require that you be very familiar with the museum and its exhibits, so be sure to do your home-work.

▼ *Be polite and cordial.* If you're working with children, remember to keep it fun and address them on a level they can understand.

▼ *Be respectful: New York has an enormous tourist trade, and you may be confronted with a variety of languages and dialects.* It's a good idea to use maps to visually point out answers to questions that don't transcend the language barrier.

▼ *Be flexible: Exhibits, schedules, and sometimes assignments will vary.* And you must have a strong sense of commitment, because many institutions take a lot of time and effort to train their volunteers.

The Listings

The listings below include some of the city's museums, botanical gardens, and galleries, and a host of other cultural institutions. But our list is by no means exhaustive. Try consulting a guidebook for the names of major institutions we've omitted. And there are many small community theater groups throughout the city, as well as public radio and television stations. (We cite a couple of examples of public broadcasting.) Programs range in size from 900 volunteers (at the American Museum of Natural History) to 16 people (at the Cloisters) to three volunteer stagehands (at a local theater group).

Listings

ABIGAIL ADAMS SMITH MUSEUM
421 E. 61st St.
New York, NY 10021
Contact: Laurie Brown, Volunteer Coordinator
(212) 838-6878

Hidden among the Upper East Side high rises, this small museum sits in a house built in the 1700s that resembles an 1820s hotel. Volunteers are trained to work as docents, to guide visitors through the museum or to answer questions. Good interpersonal skills are necessary. Shifts run four hours, and volunteers are asked to do at least one shift per week. Interview, references.

AMERICAN CRAFTS MUSEUM
40 W. 53rd St.
New York, NY 10019
Contact: Elizabeth Reiss, Director of Education
(212) 459-0926

If you're interested in crafts, this is your chance to help in the nation's foremost museum in the field. It focuses on works made from ceramics, fiber, glass, metal, and wood. There is a training program for docents, who help educate children and adults. The museum also has volunteers on call who help with mailings, fund-raisers, and various other projects. Opportunities are also found in the development department, administration, and the gift shop. Interview; training where necessary.

AMERICAN MUSEUM OF THE MOVING IMAGE
35th Avenue at 36 Street
Astoria, New York 11106
Contact: Volunteer Coordinator
(718) 784-4620

Located at the site of the historic Astoria Studios, once called the "Hollywood of the East," the American Museum of the Moving Image is dedicated to the art, history, and technology of film, television, and digital media. The museum houses the nation's largest collection of film and television artifacts and screens more than 300 films annually in its state-of-the-art facilities. Volunteers are needed to assist at the admissions desk, in the Museum shop, and on a periodic basis in the museum's administrative offices. Interview.

AMERICAN MUSEUM OF NATURAL HISTORY
Central Park West at 79th St.
New York, NY 10024
Contact: Volunteer Office
(212) 769-5566

Want to work side by side with a 50-foot dinosaur? The American Museum of Natural History is a world-renowned institution featuring some 30 million artifacts and specimens and 41 exhibit rooms—and utilizing over 900 volunteers. A truly significant part of the museum, volunteers fall into two categories. You can work with the public—at the information desk, showing children display carts with objects in the galleries, as a tour guide (training classes for tour guides won't be available again until 1997), as an explainer in a particular hall, or assisting in the new Expedition Program, which lets visitors locate various items on an "expedition" through the museum.

Or, you can be a behind-the-scenes volunteer working in the scientific departments, for the museum's magazine, or in the tour or education areas. Résumé, two interviews, training, orientation. Perks may include certain discounts, parties, special tours, and trips to other museums.

ANNABELLA GONZALEZ DANCE THEATER
4 E. 89th St.
New York, NY 10128
Contact: Annabella Gonzalez
(212) 722-4128

Annabella welcomes hardworking volunteers with an appreciation for dance. The company, which features "modern dance with a Latin touch," performs all around the city. Volunteers host galas and special events as well as helping with costume making and preparation. They are also needed to help with typing and mailings.

BLACK FASHION MUSEUM
155 W. 126th St.
New York, NY 10027
Contact: Cedric Washington
(212) 666-1320

Founded in 1979 by Lois K. Alexander, the Black Fashion Museum displays and preserves costumes from Black theater and films. The museum, the only one of its kind, even has its own television show on Manhattan's Channel 34. Volunteers with an interest in fashion might enjoy helping with day-to-day operations, cataloguing, assisting with exhibits, working in the thrift shop, or serving as tour guides. Interview.

THE BRONX MUSEUM OF THE ARTS
1040 Grand Concourse
Bronx, NY 10456
Contact: Volunteer Coordinator
(718) 681-6181

A host of exhibits and programs make up this Bronx institution, and you can be involved as a volunteer. Dedicated adult volunteers can assist in various public programs, in the administrative offices, or in educating youngsters. Interview.

BROOKLYN HISTORICAL SOCIETY
128 Pierrepont St.
Brooklyn, NY 11201
Contact: Ask for the department of interest—education, territorial, or library.
(718) 624-0890

The society is home to the Brooklyn History Museum, which is rich with Brooklyn lore including Dodgers baseball memorabilia, the set of *The Honeymooners*, and exhibits from the Navy Yard, Brooklyn Bridge, and Coney Island. If Brooklyn is your stomping ground you might enjoy giving a few hours a week to teach children about the borough's vast history. Volunteers also assist in the library, help with administrative duties, or work in the territorial department. Interview.

CHINA INSTITUTE IN AMERICA
125 E. 65th St.
New York, NY 10021
Contact: Willow H. Chang, Curator
(212) 744-8181 ext. 146

Founded in 1926, the gallery strives to bring Chinese culture to the American audience through exhibitions including Chinese folk art and ancient art. Volunteers work in three-hour shifts; they show visitors around the gallery and answer questions regarding the exhibits. Volunteer security guards are also welcome. Those interested should provide a résumé. Interview, training sessions, volunteers' meetings.

THE CLOISTERS MUSEUM
Fort Tryon Park
New York, NY 10040
Contact: Michael Norris
(212) 923-3700

Are you a "knight" person?

A branch of the Metropolitan Museum of Art, the Cloisters exhibits medieval art and architecture. Located in upper Manhattan, this is a fabulous haven away from the hustle and bustle of Midtown. Volunteers give gallery programs (better known as guided tours) to elementary school children. There's a long training period, and volunteers are asked to stay for a three-year stint, but you need only give one 90-minute tour a week and meet once a month for further training. You can contact the museum directly or try the volunteer office at the Metropolitan Museum of Art. Unfortunately, only a few volunteers are used. Interview.

COOPER-HEWITT NATIONAL MUSEUM OF DESIGN
2 E. 91st St.
New York, NY 10128
Contact: Marla Musick, Volunteer Coordinator
(212) 860-6868

One of the two Smithsonian museums in New York City (the other being the Museum of the American Indian), the Cooper-Hewitt focuses on design and the study of design. Displays cover industrial design, jewelry, fabrics, and even wallpaper. Also well known for its decorative-arts collection, the museum has an active corps of about 85 volunteers to help out everywhere from the information desk to the administrative areas. Volunteers help acquaint visitors with the museum and familiarize them with exhibits. Interview.

THE FRENCH INSTITUTE
22 E. 60th St.
New York, NY 10022
Contact: Mary Jo Palencia
(212) 355-6100, ext. 250

This French cultural and language center offers volunteer programs in its library and other areas dealing with the public. Library volunteers work at the circulation desk and help with office work. "On the Spot" volunteers are on call for special projects and mailings. You can also help as an usher, by answering phones, or at the reception desk. (French is a must for a position at the reception desk.) Interview, training.

THE FRICK COLLECTION
1 E. 70th St.
New York, NY 10021
Contact: Volunteer Coordinator
(212) 288-0700

The Frick Collection is a museum that sits in a historic home on the corner of Fifth Avenue and 70th Street. The museum attracts a large international clientele, and bilingual volunteers are a plus. Volunteers to provide information, answer questions, and work the membership desk are sought, as is supplemental help in the museum bookstore. The Frick asks for volunteers who can commit to one day a week (four hours) for a year. You will receive an orientation and reading materials about the facility. Interview.

THE HORTICULTURAL SOCIETY OF NEW YORK
128 W. 58th St.
New York, NY 10019
Contact: Volunteer Projects Coordinator
(212) 757-0915

Brightening the quality of city life through horticulture, the Horticultural Society uses volunteers in its community program, membership program, greenhouse shop, library, and offices. It also utilizes some 250 volunteers annually at the New York Flower Show. There are other special events as well. Interview.

IRISH HISTORICAL SOCIETY
991 Fifth Ave.
New York, NY 10028
Contact: Rose Meehan
(212) 288-2263

The 100 + -year-old society's goal is to make better known the Irish chapter in American history. You can help it succeed by assisting in detailed and extensive research and library work. A wonderful opportunity, especially for Irish Americans, to study and learn about Irish-American culture, while helping the society continue to grow and better serve the community. Interview, orientation.

THE JAPAN SOCIETY
333 E. 47th St.
New York, NY 10017
Contact: Volunteer Coordinator
(212) 832-1155

The Japan Society is devoted to bettering relations between the United States and Japan through culture, education, public affairs, discussions, and various programs. It is a membership organization; volunteers help out with several programs, including the outreach program and library research. The society also offers traditional and modern Japanese performing arts. As a volunteer you can usher or take tickets at these special events—and enjoy some marvelous entertainment. Interview.

THE JEWISH MUSEUM
1109 Fifth Ave.
New York, NY 10128
Contact: Mera Schwartz, Coordinator of Volunteer Programs
(212) 423-3208

You can join a volunteer staff (members) of over 200 working in this long-standing, recently renovated Manhattan museum dedicated to Jewish art and culture. Volunteers work everywhere—the gift shop, the information desk, the membership desk, the offices, the archives, and the resource center. Interview, references.

LOWER EAST SIDE TENEMENT MUSEUM
97 Orchard St.
New York, NY 10128
Contact: Renée Epps, Director of Administration
(212) 421-0233

Located on New York's Lower East Side, this relatively new historical museum interprets and preserves the neighborhood's wide variety of immigrant experiences. Volunteers can work as gallery docents, giving tours and explaining the exhibits to the public. Weekday volunteers can work with visiting school groups or help with administrative duties or fundraising. Résumé and cover letter, interview.

LOWER MANHATTAN CULTURAL COUNCIL
1 World Trade Center
Suite 1717
New York, NY 10048
Contact: Christopher Gillespie
(212) 432-0900

Many college students and young people interested in the arts volunteer and intern at this cultural facility. They promote a number of special events, such as Women in Jazz and other performances. You might get involved in the council's special events, such as the Buskers Fare, a week-long annual festival featuring street performers and using a number of volunteers to coordinate activities throughout lower Manhattan. Other volunteers help with LMCC general office work on computers. Résumé with cover letter, interview.

METROPOLITAN MUSEUM OF ART
Fifth Ave. & 82nd St.
New York, NY 10028
Contact: Rita Hurson, Volunteer Coordinator
(212) 879-5500, ext. 3738

The Met is an extremely popular setting for volunteers, with over 900 people donating their time, and usually about another 500 applications on tap. This doesn't mean you should give up—it just may not be an opportunity that will happen overnight.

The Met's programs have volunteers putting in anywhere from five days a week to a few hours on weekends. For the volunteer who holds a nine-to-five job, the Met does have a full weekend program with people staffing the information desks and visitor center and giving tours. There are also administrative jobs, available primarily on weekdays. The Met's educational opportunities are terrific for teachers and others who enjoy enlightening visitors of all ages. Interview, training.

MUSEUM OF THE CITY OF NEW YORK
103rd St. & Fifth Ave.
New York, NY 10029
Contact: Lia Miller, Volunteer Coordinator
(212) 534-1672

If you love the Big Apple, you may want to work at the Museum of the City of New York. Volunteers are placed on an individual basis throughout the various departments. There are research opportunities, a docent program, and a weekend program. There is also an ongoing need for clerical help. Applicants should send a résumé. Interview, references, training.

THE NATIONAL ACADEMY OF DESIGN
1083 Fifth Ave.
New York, NY 10019
Contact: Leslie Kurtz, Volunteer Coordinator
(212) 369-4880

A school for design as well as a museum, the academy offers you the chance to work in a prestigious environment inside a luxurious Manhattan townhouse. Docents lead tours of the academy. They also help with "Family Day" activities. Volunteers are needed primarily on weekdays, and you will be asked to do at least one 60-minute tour weekly plus attend meetings. Interview.

NEW YORK CITY BALLET
New York State Theater
Lincoln Center for the Performing Arts
New York, NY 10023-6971
Contact: Joan Quatrano, Volunteer Administrator
(212) 870-5666
Lincoln Center is home to one of the world's foremost ballet companies. As a volunteer you can assist with audience development, help administratively, or train as a docent to give preperformance talks and educate new audiences about the art form. Although hours and schedules vary depending on the activity, the company does ask for a strong ongoing commitment from all volunteers. Interview, training.

THE NEW YORK PHILHARMONIC
Lincoln Center Plaza
New York, NY 10023-6971
Contact: Leave information for the membership chairperson.
(212) 875-5755
The New York Philharmonic uses volunteers (members) to help with special fund-raising events such as opening-night galas. Looking to volunteers as liaisons to the public, the Philharmonic has them help with audience development and speak with subscribers in "user-friendly ways." The Philharmonic also allows you to volunteer in educational programs or assisting the staff. Schedules vary and include weekdays, evenings, and weekends. Interview, membership process, training.

QUEENS HISTORICAL SOCIETY
Kingsland Homestead
143-35 37th Ave.
Flushing, NY 11354
Contact: Ask for volunteer coordinator.
(718) 939-0647

The historical society operates out of an 18th-century farm-house in a small park in Flushing, Queens alongside a living landmark in the form of a 150-year-old weeping beech tree. In this small, quaint setting volunteers work as docents, do research, help in the garden or staff the reception desk. A nice opportunity for someone who doesn't want to be one of hundreds of volunteers in one of the larger institutions. Interview, orientation.

QUEENS MUSEUM OF ART
NYC Building
Flushing Meadows—Corona Park
Flushing, NY 11368
Contact: Barry Brown
(718) 592-9700, ext. 245

Located in a building originally constructed for the 1939 World's Fair, and part of the 1964–65 fair as well, the museum features a miniature version of the entire five boroughs that make up the City of New York. Films, talks, lectures, family programs, and exhibits are also part of the institute. Volunteers work as docents, in the gift shop, on special events, and in administration, including education and public information. Interview.

QUEENS THEATER IN THE PARK
P.O. Box 520069
Flushing, NY 11352
Contact: Muriel Abbott
(718) 760-0064

This performing-arts center in Flushing Meadows—Corona Park features theatrical presentations (including children's theater) plus dance, music, and film. Volunteers can help with office work and mailings or as ushers. It's a great opportunity if you have an interest in the arts . . . and an even better opportunity if you're also from Queens. Interview.

THE SOLOMON R. GUGGENHEIM MUSEUM
1071 Fifth Ave.
New York, NY 10028
Contact: Diane Maas, Volunteer Coordinator
(212) 423-3648

Reopened in 1992, the Guggenheim is one of New York's more spectacular museums to visit and to work in. Volunteer opportunities are available in every department depending on your background, interest, and availability. Positions range from working the front desk to doing research to entering the docent program (nine-month training course). It's recommended that you be familiar with the Guggenheim. Interview, references.

NOTE: Those in the Soho area might choose to volunteer at the Guggenheim Museum Soho 575 Broadway at Prince Street. Phone: (212) 423-3500

SOUTH STREET SEAPORT MUSEUM
12 Fulton St.
New York, NY 10038
Contact: Patricia Sands, Director of Volunteer Programs
(212) 669-9400

This popular museum comprises a dozen blocks, transformed into an 18th- and 19th-century seaport. It's a fun place to meet visitors and enjoy the shops; you can also put in a few hours a week as a volunteer doing anything from cataloging to providing visitors information to assisting with ship restoration and boatbuilding. Each of the many opportunities requires a different time commitment, and some require more training than others. Formal interview process.

STATEN ISLAND CHILDREN'S MUSEUM
1000 Richmond Terrace
Staten Island, NY 10301-9910
Contact: Lucia Morgan, Volunteer Coordinator
(718) 273-2060

This nonprofit museum, designed for children ages 2 through 12, offers participatory exhibits with themes in the arts, sciences, and humanities. It's a fun-filled location for visitors and volunteers alike. You can assist with school groups, answer questions, interpret exhibits, set up and clean up, help with weekend workshops, guide the many summer-camp groups that visit the facility, or act as a public greeter at the museum's front desk. Interview, training.

STATEN ISLAND INSTITUTE OF ARTS AND SCIENCES
75 Stuyvesant Place
Staten Island, NY 10301
Contact: Maria Fiorelli, Vice President, Lifelong Learning Department
(718) 727-1135

The institute is the oldest general museum on Staten Island, featuring a strong science collection, fine arts, and ample archives with thousands of photos, diaries, and letters. Volunteers work in the science and education departments, perform research in the library or archives, and assist teachers with the children's classes and in administrative areas. Contact the department in which you are interested. Interview.

THIRTEEN/WNET
356 W. 58th St.
New York, NY 10019
Contact: Suzi Leiter, Director, Volunteer Administration
(212) 560-2706

Channel 13 has been serving the New York area for over 30 years as part of the Public Broadcasting System, presenting everything from *Sesame Street* to classical concert performances to nature and science programming without commercial interruption.

During the day, as a volunteer you can be involved in almost any aspect of the station from office support to the speakers' bureau, Thirteen Talks. Volunteers also work as researchers for program producers. Then, of course, there are the twice-yearly pledge drives. They use approximately 100 volunteers, including groups working together from corporations or organizations. Interview, training, orientation.

USO OF METRO NEW YORK
151 W. 51st St.
New York, NY 10036
Contact: Ann Jarosz, Volunteer Coordinator
(212) 719-2364

The USO provides programs for active military personnel either residing in or visiting New York. Like Bob Hope, you can help entertain the troops by distributing tickets for sporting and theater events, assisting with hotel accommodations, and providing tours of the Big Apple. The USO has three offices, one in midtown Manhattan and two at Kennedy Airport. To apply you need only fill out a brief questionnaire and meet with the coordinator. No prior military training required. Orientation.

THE WHITNEY MUSEUM OF AMERICAN ART
945 Madison Ave.
New York, NY 10021
Contact: Elise Pustilnik
(212) 570-3641

One of New York's most popular museums, the Whitney provides a host of opportunities for those who want to work in this cultural atmosphere. Opportunities include assisting at the membership desk or acting as a volunteer lecturer. There is an extensive docent-training program as well. The museum is open two nights a week for those who wish to volunteer after their workday. Interview, orientation, training.

WNYC COMMUNICATIONS GROUP
1 Centre St.
New York, NY 10007
Contact: Judith Osofsky, WNYC Membership Department
(212) 669-7715

If you'd like to work in radio, WNYC provides two opportunities under one roof—WNYC–AM and WNYC–FM. On the air since 1924, these stations remain a fixture of New York broadcasting thanks to the help of volunteers like yourselves. You can help with fund-raising, special events, or office work; you can answer telephone pledge calls during the thrice-yearly fund-raising drives. Interview, résumé, training, orientation.

2

Zoos, Parks, and Other Outdoor Opportunities

Volunteering in a metropolis doesn't mean you have to be tucked away within the confines of a cultural, educational, or medical facility. Instead you might opt for an outdoor experience working with plants or animals. New York City has nearly 27,000 acres of parkland, including some 800 playgrounds and 28 recreational centers. There are gardens, zoos, and plenty of other ways for you to volunteer outdoors.

For those with a green thumb, there are planting and gardening opportunities. This can be a wonderful way to volunteer as a family. For those who enjoy animals, there are opportunities to educate youngsters—and adults, for that matter—about a variety of species at the city's zoos.

Besides cleanup and planting projects, park volunteers can help with fund-raising projects, organize special events, teach or supervise recreational activities, give tours, and help in the nature centers and environmental efforts of the city's parks. Also a key part of community unity, parks are a source of pride. And they provide a wealth of opportunities for volunteers to meet each other and work together.

Tips for "Outdoor" Volunteers

▼ *Dress appropriately.* Consider bringing sunblock, shades, and a hat. You might also bring a change of clothes: A busy volunteer is a dirty volunteer.
▼ *Consider health and allergy concerns before digging and planting or working with animals.*
▼ *If you're teaching, try not to overeducate.* Just because you took a nine-week training course doesn't mean you need to give a class of third-graders the benefit of nine weeks' worth of notes.

Enjoy the great outdoors!

Listings

We've listed the borough volunteer coordinators first, as they are the experts on the parks in each borough and can often help you find the volunteer opportunity you're looking for.

The Bronx: Valerie Davis-O'Neal,
   (718) 430-1867
Brooklyn: Voy Moore,
   (718) 965-8917
Manhattan: Mary Price,
   (212) 408-0214

Queens: Leslie Orr,
   (718) 520-5948
Staten Island: Janet Mahoney,
   (718) 390-8033

ALLEY POND ENVIRONMENTAL CENTER
228-06 Northern Blvd.
Douglaston, NY 11363
Contact: Registrar
(718) 229-4000

If you like animals you might like working at the Alley Pond Environmental Center, where a minizoo affords you the opportunity to feed, weigh, and take care of small animals such as rabbits and guinea pigs. The zoo can also use help with cleanup work, trail work, office tasks, and conservation projects. Or you can teach youngsters about animals or work with them on crafts projects. The center is open seven days a week. Interview.

THE BRONX ZOO
THE INTERNATIONAL WILDLIFE CONSERVATION PARK
Bronx, NY 10460
Contact: Carol Ferster
(718) 220-5141

No, you can't work directly with the animals, but you can watch them in action and enjoy this fabulous zoo while volunteering in any number of interesting areas. Through the educational program you can give guided tours to school groups, church groups, Scout groups, and so on. Volunteers take a twelve-week training course, which meets once a week (including weekend classes). You do need to pass the course, which is graded and includes homework—*so study!* Also, volunteers work information tables, answer letters from schoolchildren, and provide general information to the public. Training, more training, interview.

BROOKLYN BOTANICAL GARDEN
1000 Washington Ave.
Brooklyn, NY 11225
Contact: Joanne Woodfin, Volunteer Coordinator
(718) 622-4433

Over 300 volunteers put in more than 30,000 hours annually to help keep this garden—set right in the middle of Brooklyn—magnificent. You can get involved in this glorious setting for a few hours weekly by working in the library, the membership department, the planting program, or the horticultural department. On weekends you can lead special theme tours through the gardens. The annual Cherry Blossom Festival uses 60 volunteers; other special events are also held. The staff will help you find the work that best matches your interests. Interview.

CENTRAL PARK
Contact: Rowena Saunders or Lavonia Brachwaite
(212) 360-2751

One of the world's largest, most exciting parks (840 acres) offers a wealth of activities for visitors and a number of opportunities for volunteers. You can rake, clean up, paint benches, and generally help beautify the area. Offices within the park use volunteers for clerical work. There are daily and weekly programs, as well as family days and annual events such as Cleanup Day. Schedules are flexible and you can work in many places in the magnificent park. Volunteers also help out with free workshops for kids, and assist in the two park information booths. A great place for families to volunteer together. Orientation.

THE CENTRAL PARK WILDLIFE CENTER
830 Fifth Ave.
New York, NY 10023
Contact: April Rivkin, Volunteer Coordinator
(212) 439-6500

If you're seeking the "wild" life in midtown Manhattan, this is the opportunity for you. The Wildlife Conservation Society's volunteer program at Central Park offers activities for school groups, classes for children and families, and minitalks for visitors. Volunteers teach schoolchildren and other visitors about animals, offer educational information about conservation, wildlife, and the environment, get involved in special events, and, best of all, they have fun. Now celebrating its 100th anniversary, the center looks for individuals over 18 who enjoy working with children and visitors from all over the world (foreign language skills are a plus). There is a 10-

week training program, and you are asked for a one-year commitment of at least two full days per month. Interview.

FLUSHING MEADOWS–CORONA PARK
Olmsted Center
Flushing, NY 11368
Contact: Kathy Dallojacono, Director of Volunteers
(718) 760-6561

The site of New York's last two world's fairs and home to the U.S. Open tennis championship, this Queens park has several annual special-event days when volunteers can work together to clean up, plant shrubs, and beautify the park. Also, groups are welcome to make special arrangements to volunteer. Boy Scout and Girl Scout troops, as well as other groups, arrange to come to the park for a day of planting trees, raking leaves, or other activities. Administrative opportunities—such as working on mailings for park events—are also available. You need only call for information.

FOREST PARK
Oak Ridge 1 Forest Park
Woodhaven, NY 11421-1166
Contact: Debby Kuha, Director of Volunteers
(718) 235-4151

This massive wooded park on Woodhaven Boulevard in Queens has various opportunities for nature lovers to get out and plant, clean up, and help with special events. Special days, such as April's Green Up Day, and Operation Clean Sweep, are opportunities for many volunteers to get down and dirty. School groups and classes of learning-disabled students help with mailings and other duties for the park's relatively new volunteer department. The Friends of Forest Park group has nearly 250 members who help clean up after special seasonal events such as the Halloween Walk, Victorian Christmas, and so on. Potential volunteers need only call and fill out an application.

FRIENDS OF FORT TRYON PARK
P.O. Box 8666
JAS Station
New York, NY 10116-8666
Contact: Write to Friends of Fort Tryon Park Volunteers at the above address.

This beautiful upper Manhattan park is home to the fabulous Cloisters. Tourists visit from around the world, and this 500-member organization, in conjunction with the city's Parks Department, is dedicated to beautifying the park and keeping it safe, clean, and ecologically sound. Members put together a calendar of events, raise funds for various activities, and act as advocates for the park. Interested volunteers will receive an application and information about joining; there are some dues involved.

THE GREEN GUERILLAS
625 Broadway
Second Floor
New York, NY 10012
Contact: Phil Tietz, Volunteer Coordinator
(212) 674-8124

A wonderfully named community gardening organization, around for nearly 25 years, the Guerillas have about 350 active volunteers involved in all aspects of community gardening, from clearing lots to planting gardens in all five boroughs. They make pocket parks out of vacant lots—and you can help. There are monthly orientations for new volunteers; once involved you can be listed on the computer and are sent information on upcoming opportunities and events. Most activities take place in the evening and on weekends. Office volunteers welcome as well. Orientation.

THE NEW YORK AQUARIUM
W. 8th St. & First Ave.
Brooklyn, NY 11224
Contact: Barbara Schioppa, Volunteer Coordinator
(718) 265-3450

You can help greet and educate some of the aquarium's

800,000 annual visitors as a volunteer explaining the numerous exhibits. Fifteen hours of training classes are required, after which you will be stationed at an exhibit, where you will inform the public and answer questions. If you are articulate, interested in science, and enjoy speaking to large groups of adults and even larger groups of children about animals, animal biology, and conservation, this is an ideal opportunity. Volunteers are asked to put in a minimum of 15 hours per month. Interview, training.

PROSPECT PARK
95 Prospect Park West
Brooklyn, NY 11215
Contact: Prospect Park Volunteers Office
(718) 965-8960

Prospect Park offers a wealth of horticultural opportunities for outdoors lovers. The Woodlands Management program offers volunteers the chance to do forest restoration and other renovations. Volunteers are also used for special events, and they assist with the park's cultural programs. The park offers monthly volunteer orientation sessions.

See also chapter 6, "Families."

RIVERSIDE PARK FUND
475 Riverside Park
Room 249
New York, NY 10115
Contact: Park Fund

The fund, less than a decade old, has made a tremendous impact on the welfare of Riverside Park. You, as a volunteer, can lend a hand with planting, sweeping, cleaning up, weeding, or working in the office. Interested parties should call. Interview.

SALT MARSH RESTORATION TEAM
200 Nevada Ave.
Staten Island, NY 10306
Contact: Robbin Bergfors
(718) 667-7477

Zoos, Parks . . .

One of the more significant conservation projects in New York, this organization is dedicated to cleaning up and restoring the areas of Staten Island's waterways devastated by the oil spill at the start of the decade. The project, which will continue at least through October 1996, uses volunteers for planting and restoring the region's natural habitat. Several planting weekends will be scheduled in the spring and summer. This is a terrific way to spend time outdoors away from the office, helping the environment in a hands-on manner.

STATEN ISLAND BOTANICAL GARDEN
1000 Richmond Terrace
Staten Island, NY 10301
Contact: Laura Graham, Director of Development
(718) 273-8200, ext. 11

Volunteers help with garden planting and maintenance, assist in the conservatory with plant sales, and give tours. The compost center, which recycles organic materials, is very popular in these ecologically aware times. There are also opportunities to volunteer in the gift shop, lecturing, running workshops, or helping with special events. Interview, training, and supervision in your area of interest.

STATEN ISLAND ZOO
Barrett Park
614 Broadway
Staten Island, NY 10310
Contact: Regina Pistilli, Coordinator of Docents and Volunteers
(718) 442-3101

Yes, you can work with the animals, holding them as children pet them. To do so you must have rabies shots and a TB test, as nonhuman mammals can catch TB. There is also a docent-training program, which lasts ten weeks and prepares you to give tours and answer questions about the facility. For weekday workers/weekend warriors there is a weekend program. There are other ongoing needs to fill, including keeping the science library up-to-date and seeking out new books to augment the library. The zoo also offers clerical opportunities as well as special-event volunteer options, including decorating the zoo for Halloween, pumpkin carving, and more. Interview, references, training.

Other related numbers you might want to call include:

City Parks Foundation,
(212) 360-1399

For information on volunteering in one of the city's many historic houses/museums.

Historical House Trust,
(212) 360-8123,

Other Friends of the Parks groups include:

Central Park Conservancy,
(212) 315-0385 (Manhattan)
Friends of Van Cortlandt Park,
(718) 430-1890 (Bronx)
Greenbelt Conservancy,
(718) 667-2165 (Staten
Island)

Prospect Park Alliance,
(718) 965-8951 (Brooklyn)
Randalls Island Sports
Foundation, (212) 830-7715

3

Children

Whereas many of the listings in this book involve working with children (whether in community centers, Y's, hospitals, or educational facilities), this section focuses directly on services for children. There are numerous volunteer opportunities to educate our city's young people and enhance their cultural, social, and academic lives.

Working with youngsters takes a sense of commitment. Children need stability and like to see a familiar face, be it once or twice a week or once a month. Many of the children who need services have been disappointed too many times before, and they certainly don't want to make a new connection unless they sense that you will be there for them. Of course, your job is not to right the wrongs created by society, dysfunctional families, or educational budget cuts. Your job is to inspire kids, set a positive example, and guide them through athletic or educational activities.

What Makes a Good Volunteer with Children?

The ability to relate to kids on their level while remaining a figure of respect and authority. A good sense of *fun* helps too.

You will be assuming a role as a tutor, coach, mentor, or Big Brother or Big Sister. The most effective volunteers are those who relate to kids in a way they can understand. Know their likes and dislikes; be tuned in to their world. Effectively working with children means effectively communicating with them and applying your skills, knowledge, and expertise to help break through the barriers of communication.

Other Tips for Working with Children

▼ *Be consistent and reliable.*
▼ *Don't expect more than they can give.* You don't want to become one of those overzealous Little League coaches expecting an undefeated season and a team full of Ken Griffey, Jrs. Be aware of a child's physical abilities and limitations, and always be sensitive to their cognitive and emotional levels.
▼ *Let children be children.* (They get dirty once in a while.)
▼ *Be able to say* no *when you have to, but do not take on the role of disciplinarian or overstep your boundaries.* Take any problems that may arise to your administrator.

Working with children takes common sense, alertness, consistency, warmth, energy, sincerity, understanding, and a penchant for having fun.

Listings

Here they are! Also see chapters 6, 7, and 12, for more opportunities to volunteer with young people in New York.

BOY SCOUTS OF AMERICA
NEW YORK CITY CHAPTER
345 Hudson St.
New York, NY 10014
Contact: Ask for borough executive in your area.
Main Number (212) 242-1100, ext. 324

Over 2,000 Cub Packs and Boy Scout Troops make up the New York area contingent. You can head one such pack or troop as a volunteer Boy Scout Troop Leader. Junior leaders are 18 to 21, and senior troop leaders must be over 21 and work well with kids. If you enjoy a wide range of outdoor (and some indoor) activities, you might want to get involved. Troops meet weekly. Interview, orientation, training.

CAMP FRIENDSHIP YOUTH PROGRAMS
339 E. 8th St.
Brooklyn, NY 11215
Contact: John Duda, Director
(718) 965-3695

Camp Friendship offers educational and recreational opportunities to the underprivileged children of southern Brooklyn. If you would like to be a sports coach or a tutor and you work well with youngsters and teens, this might be up your alley. Other volunteers help with fund-raising events and mailings. Interview.

CATHOLIC BIG BROTHERS
45 E. 20th St.
New York, NY 10003
Contact: Sandy Maskell, Program Coordinator
(212) 477-2250

Both boys and girls can benefit from having someone in their life acting as a mentor and positive role model.

As a Big Brother or Big Sister, you will spend part of your weekend taking a child (age 7–17) to cultural events, movies, sporting events, etc. There are also agency functions in which to participate. It's a rewarding experience to make a difference in the life of a child through educational and recreational means. Lengthy interview, three written references, background check, home visit, screening, training.

CHILD ABUSE PREVENTION PROGRAM OF NEW YORK
2 MetroTech Center
Brooklyn, NY 11201
Contact: Angela Cayle, Program Director
(718) 834-6655

For over ten years, the Child Abuse Prevention Program (CAPP) has been teaching elementary school children how to identify and report instances of sexual and physical abuse. Using life-sized puppets to create skits and scenarios that explore abusive situations, CAPP provides educational and intervention services to 8- to 10-year-olds in all five boroughs. You can help support this marvelous program by assisting in their fund-raising efforts and by helping to set up the program in new schools. CAPP also sponsors letter-writing campaigns to politicians and lobbies for children's rights. Interview, training sessions, monthly meetings.

CHRISTIAN CHILDREN'S ASSOCIATION
3022 Olinville Ave.
Bronx, NY 10467
Contact: Vilma Young, Director and Founder
(718) 652-2524

This association's performing arts program looks for weekend tutors to work with elementary and high school students in the performing arts, including poetry, drama, and choral programs for international television. Teen volunteers (14 and over) are also encouraged to get involved in helping their community. The association looks to motivate teens and even gives national service awards to those who best exemplify constructive role models. Interview, orientation.

COVENANT HOUSE
346 W. 17th St.
New York, NY 10011
Contact: Erin Gallivan, Volunteer Coordinator
(212) 727-4917

Covenant House provides services for homeless children 21 and under through two shelters and long-term independent-living programs. They have several locations throughout the city and you can help in the kitchen, taking care of babies, assisting with recreation and outreach programs, and much more. Covenant House is open 24 hours a day, every day, and the need for volunteers is ongoing. Interview, two references, state child abuse clearance.

FRESH AIR FUND
1040 Avenue of the Americas
New York, NY 10022
Contact: Francine Beauregard, Volunteer Coordinator
(212) 221-0900

If you loved camp, here's your chance to help a child who otherwise might not get in on the fun. The Fresh Air Fund helps kids go to summer camp. It also has programs that send children from the five boroughs away to spend time with families in other states or even in Canada. Your help is valuable in making outreach phone calls to parents, with administrative work, and in helping counselors with special weekend trips. You can even be a day counselor. There is also an opportunity for volunteers to help the benefit committee work on the annual fund-raiser. Interview, references.

FRIENDS OF THE PUBLIC SCHOOLS
280 Broadway
Suite 737
New York, NY 10007
Contact: Lois Rivkin, President
(212) 349-6907

Serving as a liaison between the students and New York's business, cultural, and civic sectors, Friends of the Public Schools offers unique and diverse ways of getting involved on a schedule that works for you, in your field of interest or expertise. Chefs and culinary experts give classes in cooking; artists help youngsters develop their artistic talents; lawyers enhance students' knowledge of the legal arena with moot court trials—you name it. There is no set pattern by which volunteers get involved. This is a wonderful "out of the class-room" way to get in touch with the city's youth in all five boroughs. Interview, screening.

GIRLS CLUB OF NEW YORK
1130 Grand Concourse
Bronx, NY 10456
Contact: Frank Morales, Jr., Executive Director
(718) 590-4050

For the past 40 years the Girls Club of New York has been committed to serving and helping young people in the inner city. The South Bronx facility features a number of clubs and programs for girls from ages 6 to 21. Volunteers are sought for after-school programs. Responsibilities include tutoring the 6- to 12-year-olds in subjects such as math and English as well as helping with homework. The evening recreation program for 13- to 18-year-olds features clubs that meet twice a week and utilizes volunteers as club leaders. The day camp program offers over 100 girls summer fun through counselor and instructor involvement. Interview, references, screening, training.

GRAHAM-WINDHAM SERVICES TO FAMILIES
33 Irving Place
New York, NY 10003
Contact: Susan Gunn, Director of Volunteers
(212) 529-6445, ext. 320

Founded in 1806, Graham-Windham is the oldest nonsectarian foster care agency in the country. With various sites around the city, including a residence in Brooklyn, the agency helps children in foster care be placed with families and in group homes. It also works with parents and kids in preventive programs aimed at keeping parents from abusing their children so that they don't end up in foster care. Volun-

teers are used as mentors and tutors—not as counselors—in a
number of programs that help children of all ages. Interview,
state child abuse clearance, medical and personal references,
screening. Training where necessary.

THE GUILD FOR EXCEPTIONAL CHILDREN
260 68th St.
Brooklyn, NY 11220
Contact: Michael Frankewich, Executive Director
(718) 833-6633
With patience and understanding you can help the guild
provide mentally retarded children with an education and
placement in a residential program. Volunteers assist in social
recreational programs, residential programs, and preschool
and early-intervention programs. Interview, screening,
training.

HOLY TRINITY CENTER
316 E. 88th St.
New York, NY 10128
Contact: Reverend Herbert G. Draesel, Jr.
(212) 289-4100
After-school programs, a summer day camp, special holiday
dinners and Christmas Parties for children are just a few of
the activities provided by the center. In the after-school program, volunteers tutor children and help them with their
homework. The summer day camp provides activities for kids,
and the holiday parties help make the Thanksgivings and
Christmases of disadvantaged youths more festive. Interview,
training.

HOMES FOR THE HOMELESS
36 Cooper Square
Sixth Floor
New York, NY 10003
Contact: Volunteer Coordinator
(212) 529-5252
The four residences (one in each borough except Brooklyn)
provide transitional housing to homeless families. Each loca-

tion has 24-hour security and is clean and well run. Volunteers tutor the children of these families, as they often miss out on structured schooling. If you are proficient in a subject, you may consider sending a résumé and helping these kids. Interview.

See also chapter 8, "Homeless."

ISLAND ACADEMY
RIKERS ISLAND
East Elmhurst, NY 11370
Contact: Ellen Kaplan
(718) 726-6505

This is a program whereby you can provide a positive role model for a young man between the ages of 16 and 18 who has been incarcerated at Rikers Island. After an initial visit at Rikers you meet with the youth for two hours a week in the community following his release. Open to male volunteers over the age of 21, this is a rewarding experience. Interview, references, training.

JEWISH BOARD OF FAMILY AND CHILDREN'S SERVICES
Mary S. Froelich Division of Volunteer Services
120 W. 57th St.
New York, NY 10019
Contact: Volunteer Division
(212) 397-4090

As a volunteer you can become involved at one of over 70 locations providing services to families and children throughout all five boroughs. Act as a mentor, tutor, Big Brother or Big Sister, child care assistant, or therapy escort. The board offers all types of services, including counseling, tutoring, and therapeutic assistance. They use many volunteers, one of whom could be you. Interview, references, training.

See also chapter 14 "Umbrella Organizations and Referral Groups."

KIPS BAY BOYS AND GIRLS CLUB
1930 Randall Ave.
Bronx, NY 10473
Contact: Dale Drakeford, Associate Director
(718) 893-8254

If you can provide a positive role model, coach a team, or teach an athletic skill, you might want to get involved with some of the kids of Kips Bay. Volunteers serve as physical education instructors, team coaches, game room supervisors, lifeguards (with a senior life-saving certificate from the Red Cross), tutors, and bus drivers. Résumé with cover letter; interview, training.

LEFFERTS HOMESTEAD CHILDREN'S MUSEUM
Prospect Park
Flatbush Ave. and Empire Blvd.
Brooklyn, NY 11225
Contact: Prospect Park Volunteer Office
(718) 965-8960
Lefferts Homestead Children's Historic House
(718) 965-6505

The Homestead Children's Museum occupies a late-18th-century building that has been designed to resemble an early-19th-century farmhouse. At this hands-on museum, volunteer opportunities include working with children and helping them participate in activities as well as giving tours and answering questions about the facility. Interested volunteers can start by attending a volunteer orientation session held monthly by the park. Interview, training.

See also chapter 2, "Zoos, Parks, and Other Outdoor Opportunities" and chapter 6, "Families."

THE LIGHTHOUSE
111 E. 59th St.
New York, NY 10022
Contact: Carol Robbins, Director of Volunteer Services
(212) 821-9405

The Lighthouse serves visually impaired persons of all ages through direct services, research, and education, enabling people with vision impairment to be independent. One of the group's most significant programs is the Saturday Youth Program. This affords school-age children recreational and educational opportunities, and you as a volunteer can help! Interview, training.

See also chapter 12, "Health and Human Services."

McMAHON SERVICES FOR CHILDREN
305 Seventh Ave.
New York, NY 10001
Contact: Susan Kyle, Volunteer Coordinator
(212) 243-7070

Serving children since 1919, McMahon Services deals with just some of the many children in New York's foster care system. Determined to develop each child's potential to the fullest, McMahon has volunteers on hand to lead arts-and-crafts groups, play games, lead sing-alongs, tell stories, assist foster parents, and generally provide positive role models. Due to abuse, neglect, and the state's inability to improve the system through more permanent placement, most of these children are emotionally troubled. Therefore, being patient and understanding, and having the desire to brighten a child's day on a consistent basis—committing to at least three months—is also very important. Interviews, state child abuse clearance, orientation.

MADISON SQUARE BOYS AND GIRLS CLUB
301 E. 29th St.
New York, NY 10016
Contact: Leroy Branch, Volunteer Coordinator
(212) 532-5751

Through recreational, educational, and vocational services, the Madison Square Boys and Girls Club provides positive opportunities for children and teens in Manhattan, the Bronx, and Brooklyn. Tutors work with students afternoons and evenings, coaches teach activities such as volleyball and basketball and mentors offer one-on-one guidance to teens. The club asks for a minimum commitment of three hours a week. Interview, references, training, orientation.

MAKE-A-WISH FOUNDATION OF METRO NEW YORK
85 Old Shore Rd.
Port Washington, NY 11050
Contact: Kathleen Frost, Director of Volunteer Services
(212) 505-WISH

This Long Island–based foundation provides a very special service, fulfilling wishes of children who are terminally ill or suffering from life-threatening illnesses. The ultimate goal of the Make-a-Wish Foundation is that no child will ever die without a special wish fulfilled. Volunteers give their time to help make these wishes come true. Other areas in which you can help the organization include community relations, financial planning, media and public relations, and special events. Call for a volunteer application. Three references, orientation, interview, training.

MID-BRONX SENIOR CITIZENS COUNCIL
900 Grand Concourse
Bronx, NY 10451
Contact: Volunteer Coordinator
(718) 588-8200, ext. 240

The council's Youth Education, Employment, and Empowerment Services Program is designed for seniors to provide junior high school students with everything from lectures and classes to cultural awareness to fun and games. You can run workshops, teach activities such as art or dance, help with homework, or help supervise other activities for 12- to 18-year-olds. It's a "getting involved" atmosphere, weekdays 8 A.M. to 6 P.M. and Saturdays from 10 A.M. to 3 P.M.

MIND-BUILDERS CREATIVE ARTS CENTER
3415 Olinville Ave.
Bronx, NY 10467
Contact: Walter Granberry, Program Director
(718) 652-6256

This vocational and educational facility's objective is to provide support for and better the self-esteem of black and Hispanic youths. Volunteers help in the programming, operation, and administration of the center. Those with a background in public relations, advertising, and marketing help promote and market the facility, while others assist in the office with a number of functions. There are also volunteers who help with theatrical presentations. Résumé, cover letter, interview; training where necessary.

NEW YORK CITY DEPARTMENT OF JUVENILE JUSTICE
365 Broadway
New York, NY 10013
Contact: Diane McCleary, Volunteer Coordinator
(212) 925-7779, ext. 251

The DJJ provides secure as well as nonsecure detention in various locations around New York City. Volunteers tutor youngsters in various subjects and help with homework. Or, they escort children on outings and assist in special activities provided as rewards for good behavior. Evening and week-end hours are available for nine-to-fivers and a minimum of only three hours a week is asked of volunteers. Interview, screening.

NEW YORK CITY SCHOOL VOLUNTEER PROGRAM
443 Park Ave.
New York, NY 10016
Contact: Volunteer Department
(212) 213-3370

If you'd like to help out at a New York City public school near you, they'd love to have you apply.

Along with basic tutoring, there are several programs you can get involved with, including Project Homestretch, which has trained volunteers helping students stay in school and successfully complete their courses, as well as assisting with college decision making. The Authors Read Aloud Project brings children's authors into the classroom, while the Early Identification and Intervention Program identifies reading problems in young children and helps them bolster their reading ability. There is a cultural resources program, which introduces children to New York's culture by way of trips to museums, and the like. Volunteers are asked to give two or more hours a week to these or other School Volunteer Programs. Interview, training.

See also Education.

POLICE ATHLETIC LEAGUE
34½ E. 12th St.
New York, NY 10003
Contact: Mary K. DePaola, Director of Human Resources
(212) 477-9450, ext. 330

A citywide youth organization serving over 50,000 youngsters, the PAL has been active in New York City for over 80 years. There are centers in all five boroughs, providing recreational activities from sports and ballet classes to arts and crafts. Volunteer coaches and teachers must get along well with kids and have some level of proficiency at their chosen skill. Volunteers also work in the office, answering phones, typing, and so on. Interview.

See also Education.

RHEEDLEN FOUNDATION
2770 Broadway
New York, NY 10025
Contact: Regina Garrett, Volunteer Coordinator

Established in 1970, the Rheedlen Foundation is a community-based, nonprofit preventative service, working with inner city families from Harlem to Hell's Kitchen to help keep families together and children out of foster care. Six of their 12 facilities offer after-school programs, run by volunteers. Help with homework, teach crafts, and form one-on-one relationships with kids ages 5 to 12 to keep them from dropping out or becoming delinquent. Volunteers are especially needed on weekday afternoons from 3–6 to work with kids after school. A 3-hour commitment, 2 to 4 times a month. Interview, application, references, on-site training.

TALBOT PERKINS CHILDREN'S SERVICES
116 W. 32nd St.
New York, NY 10001
Contact: Karen Granby, Director of Human Resources
(212) 736-2510

Talbot Perkins provides on-site and off-site care to abused and neglected children. Services include foster care and adoption, preventive services, and substance abuse treatment. As a volunteer, you can help with activities, take care of younger children, and help adolescents prepare for independent living. There is also an ongoing need for tutors, volunteers for fund-raising activities, and helpers in the administrative offices. Interview, three references, PPD test for TB, orientation, training.

Children

4
Animals

If you're an animal lover you might decide to spend a few hours a week taking care of or helping to find good homes for the many stray animals throughout the city. They need your love and attention, too. Below are a few places in which you can help brighten the lives of our four-legged friends.

Listings

THE AMERICAN SOCIETY FOR THE PREVENTION OF CRUELTY TO ANIMALS
Volunteer Office
424 E. 92nd St.
New York, NY 10128
Contact: Volunteer Coordinator
(212) 876-7711
Volunteers are an important part of the ASPCA's programs. For those who love animals, this might be the place to spend

your volunteer hours. ASPCA volunteers get involved in humane education, animal socialization, community outreach programs, special events, and other areas. From dog walking to a dog-training apprenticeship, there are a host of opportunities. A six-hour-a-month, six-month commitment is required. The society is happy to welcome on board those who hope to make the world a more humane place for all animals. Interview, orientation, training; $25 one-year membership requirement.

BIDE-A-WEE HOMES ASSOCIATION
410 E. 38th St.
New York, NY 10016
Contact: Volunteer Coordinator
(212) 532-4986
Larger facilities in Wantagh and Westhampton.
Bide-A-Wee is a nonprofit, no-kill shelter that has been caring for animals since 1900.

Volunteers can walk the dogs, provide them with exercise, and more. For cat lovers, cleaning, socializing, and grooming are part of the program. There is also a pet therapy program, whereby you take your own pet to people in institutions such as nursing homes or facilities for the disabled and let them enjoy the company of a loving dog or cat. Volunteers and their pets are both trained for this. Volunteers are used seven days a week; clerical help is also needed. Interview, training.

THE HUMANE SOCIETY OF NEW YORK
306 E. 59th St.
New York, NY 10022
(212) 752-4840
Call for further information.

MIGHTY MUTTS
P.O. Box 140139
Brooklyn, NY 11214-0139
Contact: Heather Hallack or John Contino
(718) 946-1074
Want to help animals find homes with families to take good

care of them? Mighty Mutts not only feeds, takes in, and cares for stray animals, but also has a Saturday afternoon concession at the corner of Union Square West and 14th Street in Manhattan, where you can help as a volunteer finding homes for these animals. Saturday hours are 11 A.M. to 5 P.M.; you can help for part or all of that time.

PET OWNERS WITH AIDS RESOURCE SERVICE (POWARS)
1674 Broadway, Suite 7A
New York, NY 10019
(212) 246-6307
Contact: Steve Kohn
Founded in 1988, POWARS is a total pet care service for people with AIDS. Volunteers are needed to walk dogs, groom pets, answer phones, work the table at street fairs and cat and dog shows, and deliver pet food and supplies (people with cars a plus). Run by 450 volunteers serving about 375 pet owners, this is an excellent opportunity for animal lovers with tight schedules—no minimum time requirement and abundant opportunities in all five boroughs. Application, orientation, training seminar.

5

Education

Volunteering in a school or university can involve anything from tutoring to organizing a bake sale to joining the PTA. The school system is always in need of volunteers. Outside the school system, however, volunteers can tutor and teach courses in community centers, Y's, and other facilities throughout the five boroughs. (See Children; Community.) In parks and zoos volunteers teach children about animals, conservation, and ecology. (See Zoos, Parks, and Other Outdoor Opportunities.)

Many programs overlap into the area of education. And it's not only children who need to be educated. Immigrants want to learn English, inmates need job training, and disabled people are looking to learn new skills. Educational opportunities are quite diverse and offer volunteers numerous ways to get involved.

Why Volunteer to Educate?

One of the nicest things about the educational arena is that whether you are tutoring math or helping a homeless person learn to put together a résumé or fill out a job application, you can see the results of your efforts. Most volunteer opportunities are not as obviously gratifying. Also, tutoring, mentoring, and general equivalency diploma (GED) training are great ways to forge a strong connection. Through the shared task at hand, you will find that your relationship will transcend algebra, verbal proficiency, and other academic areas. Personalized tutoring or mentoring can build strong, meaningful bonds.

Tips on Volunteering in the Educational Arena

▼ *Know the abilities and limitations of your pupil(s).* Remember that teaching is not simply knowing a subject and talking about it to someone else, it's making sure that a connection is made so that your wisdom is absorbed.

▼ *Be aware: Don't accept a blank stare as a positive response, but don't browbeat either.* Patience is a teacher's greatest asset.

▼ *Listen, move along at the student's pace, and do your homework.* You can't teach effectively if you're not prepared.

▼ *When speaking in front of groups or classes, remember to enunciate, project your voice, and ask for questions.* People learn by asking questions, and if you're sufficiently trained, you should have most of the answers.

Listings

Many tutoring programs, courses, and classes are part of larger facilities and are therefore listed in other sections. However, we list below a number of educational opportunities ranging from tutoring children to teaching CPR to raising money for educational funding.

ACCESS FOR WOMEN
250 Jay St.
Brooklyn, NY 11201
Contact: Sybil Tabuteau
(718) 260-5730

Access for Women provides nontraditional training (in non-classroom settings) for young mothers through tutoring in areas including math, reading, writing, and various other skills. If you have a couple of hours on weekday afternoons, you can help these young women learn while they raise their children. Interview; training where necessary.

AMERICAN CANCER SOCIETY
New York City Division
19 W. 56th St.
New York, NY 10019
Contact: Anne Hecht, Personnel Services and Training Coordinator
(212) 586-8700

The American Cancer Society looks for volunteers versed in research and preventive measures to hit their lecture circuit. Volunteering isn't limited to medical personnel; you will be trained. Public speaking skills are, however, necessary. Lectures are given in various places throughout each community. Interview, training.

Volunteer opportunities are available in the other boroughs. Queens is run separately; call (718) 263-2224.

See also chapter 12, "Health and Human Services."

THE AMERICAN RED CROSS OF GREATER NEW YORK
Volunteer Resources
150 Amsterdam Ave.
New York, NY 10023
(212) 787-1000

They've been going strong for years thanks to volunteers. You, too, can be part of the Red Cross safety and health program by becoming an instructor. Volunteer instructors teach courses in treating burns, broken bones, bleeding, injuries to children, choking, and so on. You may even teach CPR. Vol-

Education

unteers also give presentations informing children, teens, and adults about HIV/AIDS. Bilingual instructors are valuable. If you like to entertain children, you can help with puppet shows that teach youngsters about fire and burn safety. There are a lot of areas in which to educate through the Red Cross. Interview, training.

See also chapter 12, "Health and Human Services."

BROOKLYN PUBLIC LIBRARY
Grand Army Plaza
Brooklyn, NY 11238
Contact: Susan O'Conner, Director, Literary Volunteers
(718) 780-7819
The literary program, offered in many of Brooklyn's branches, provides reading material and tutoring to people of all ages. In everything from English as a second language to literacy classes, you can help others enjoy the wealth of knowledge that comes from reading. You need a high school diploma or GED. Interview, training.

COUNCIL SENIOR CENTER
241 W. 72nd St.
New York, NY 10023
Contact: Gary Perkins
(212) 799-7205
Many senior centers and community centers use volunteers to teach older individuals.

This senior center welcomes midweek volunteers to teach classes in areas such as pottery, sculpture, drawing, and other forms of artistic expression. If you are proficient at a skill, can articulate it well, and have patience, you might enjoy teaching seniors. Interview, orientation.

See also chapter 7, "Community" and chapter 11, "Seniors."

HILLEL OF NEW YORK
381 Park Ave. South
Suite 613
New York, NY 10016
Contact: Wendy Levinson, Head of Volunteer Services
(212) 696-1590

Hillel strives to strengthen Jewish identity through education as well as social and cultural activities. Students may volunteer to help in the Jewish community at various community-related and fund-raising activities. Other programs include helping mildly handicapped students and even going to Israel to help immigrant children. Some 25 Hillel campus locations can be found throughout the city. Nonstudents are welcome to volunteer directly in the Hillel offices doing clerical or receptionist work. Interview.

HOPE PROGRAM I.D.
157 Montague St.
Brooklyn, NY 11201
Contact: Jon Bunge, Program and Graduate Services Director
(718) 852-9307

This program, over a decade old, provides a 14-week job readiness and life skills program for homeless and formerly homeless adults. There is also a separate GED program. Volunteers can get involved in either area as a literacy teacher or a job readiness mentor. Reliable volunteers are welcome and need only give one to two hours a week at either of the two Brooklyn locations (the other is in East New York). Interview.

INTERFAITH NEIGHBORS
247 E. 82nd St.
Third Floor
New York, NY 10028
Contact: Katherine Sorel, Education Coordinator
(212) 472-3567

Interfaith welcomes skilled volunteers—like you—to help youngsters learn about and understand the broad social realities they face and help them to maximize their social competence.

The center provides volunteer tutors for children between 10 and 15 years old in a variety of school subjects. There is also an ongoing need for volunteers to help with administrative functions in the office, to run groups, and to work on the newsletter. Communication, writing, and office skills are a plus. Interview.

LEGAL OUTREACH
433 W. 123rd St.
New York, NY 10027
Contact: Bethsheba Cooper, College Bound Director
(212) 769-7514

Legal Outreach is a legal-education organization that seeks to inspire black and Hispanic youth to pursue careers in law. Tutors proficient in math, the sciences and foreign languages (particularly Spanish and French) help high school students from 4 P.M. to 6 P.M. Monday through Thursday. Interview.

NEW YORK CITY DEPARTMENT OF CORRECTIONS
60 Hudson St.
New York, NY 10013
Room 616
Contact: Antonio McCloud, Director, Office of Volunteer Services
(212) 266-1408

If you're looking for an interesting, challenging opportunity this certainly qualifies.

The counseling unit teaches volunteers to work with inmates, helping them prepare for life after their release. Counselors assist with conflict-resolution seminars and self-esteem-building workshops. Interpersonal skills and/or a background in psychology are helpful. Volunteers also work with inmates' families and help facilitate paperwork for discharge.

Outside the facilities themselves, volunteers are needed to locate jobs for former inmates and to help place them back into the community. Often, educating the community at large about accepting former inmates is also necessary. All interested volunteers have to register with the New York City Department of Corrections Office of Volunteer Services. Once you've been given an assignment and a background check has been completed, you will be issued an identification card to work in the facilities. Volunteers are also invited to an annual award ceremony, where they receive a certificate for their work. Interview, training.

NEW YORK CITY DEPARTMENT OF JUVENILE JUSTICE
365 Broadway
New York, NY 10013
Contact: Antoinette Staffa
(212) 925-7779, ext. 303

The DJJ provides secure and nonsecure detention as well as voluntary services to help children back into school and into the community. Tutors are needed in reading, math, and other subjects including current events, and also to assist in doing homework. Day, evening and weekend hours are available in the Bronx, Manhattan, Queens, and Brooklyn. Interview.

NEW YORK CITY SCHOOL VOLUNTEER PROGRAM
443 Park Ave. South
New York, NY 10016
Contact: Volunteer Department
(212) 213-3370

If you want to help educate New York's children and work in the schools, this is the route to take. As a school volunteer you will give at least two hours a week to an elementary school, intermediate school, or high school near your home or workplace. After screening and orientation, you will help students in either reading, math, or English. In the upper grades you may prepare students for important exams and assist them in preparing for college. Some volunteers introduce children to music or art, or share their love of books. A variety of other programs are available; they have one thing in common: educating our youth. Interview, references, screening.

See also chapter 14, "Umbrella Organizations and Referral Groups."

THE NEW YORK PUBLIC LIBRARY
CENTERS FOR READING AND WRITING
Bloomingdale Regional Branch Library
150 W. 100th St.
New York, NY 10025
(212) 932-7920

The New York Public Library, serving Manhattan, the Bronx, and Staten Island, offers a comfortable place to learn and a rewarding place to volunteer. Adults 16 and over, ranging from beginning readers to pre–high school equivalency, use the library's centers days, evenings, and (at some locations) Saturdays to enhance their reading skills. Students can join tutoring groups of two to five people or attend larger classes.

Volunteer tutors need not have prior teaching experience, as they will be trained by a professional staff at each center. Students and teachers read and write together twice a week for four hours. Training workshops are held several times a year.

The following is a list of participating libraries.

In the Bronx:

Fordham Library Center,
(718) 220-6588
Francis Martin Library,
(718) 584-1980

Mott Haven Library,
(718) 665-6861
Wakefield Library,
(718) 994-8782

In Manhattan:

Harlem Library, (212) 860-7246
St. Agnes Library, (212) 787-4014

Seward Park Library,
(212) 860-7246

On Staten Island:

St. George Library Center,
(718) 816-1025

POLICE ATHLETIC LEAGUE
34¹/₂ E. 12th St.
New York, NY 10003
Contact: Mary K. DePaola, Director of Human Resources
(212) 477-9450, ext. 330

With various locations throughout the city, the PAL provides both athletic and educational opportunities to youngsters. If you can patiently and effectively tutor children age 6 through 13 in math, English, reading, writing, or spelling at least one afternoon a week, this might be right for you. Interview, screening.

See also chapter 3, "Children."

QUEENS BOROUGH PUBLIC LIBRARY
90-04 Merrick Blvd.
Jamaica, NY 11432
Contact: Gayle Cooper, Education Specialist
(718) 657-2779

This adult learning center was established nearly 20 years ago to fulfill two primary functions. It teaches reading and writing to adults with reading scores below the fifth grade level, and teaches immigrants English as a second language. To qualify you need to work well with others and have a high school diploma or GED. The program has an 18-hour training course and requires a minimum of three hours a week plus a one-year commitment. Interview.

THE SALVATION ARMY
4133 Park Ave.
New York, NY 10457
Contact: Captain Lynn Gensler
(212) 583-3500

The Salvation Army's Adult Rehabilitation Center seeks teachers for many subjects. If you would like to teach reading, math, or any number of employment-related skills to men with treatable handicaps, you need only volunteer one hour a week on a weekend or a weekday evening. Interview.

See also chapter 8, "Homeless" and chapter 12, "Health and Human Services."

SHOREFRONT YM–YWHA
300 Coney Island Ave.
Brooklyn, NY 11235
Contact: Natalie Fishman
(718) 934-3500

YMCAs and YM–YWHAs use volunteers to teach a variety of classes. One such example is the Shorefront Y, where volunteers tutor English. You can help lead small groups of new immigrants and refugees in conversational English. Applicants are interviewed and naturally must have patience and good communication skills; bilingual abilities help tremendously. A two-hour-a-week minimum commitment is required.

See also chapter 7, "Community."

STANLEY ISAACS NEIGHBORHOOD CENTER
415 E. 93rd St.
New York, NY 10128
Contact: Ira Yankwitt
(212) 360-7630

This multiservice community center meets the social, nutritional, and educational needs of low-income families in Yorkville and East Harlem. The Adult Learning Center uses volunteers to tutor adult-education students in math, writing, or English as a second language. If you possess teaching skills and are available in the evenings between 6 P.M. and 9 P.M., you might apply.

UNITED NEGRO COLLEGE FUND
500 E. 62nd St.
New York, NY 10021
Contact: Jim Wright, Project Manager
(212) 326-1225

The United Negro College Fund is a volunteer-driven national organization dedicated to enhancing educational opportunities for African-Americans. Volunteers assist with activities throughout the city to help raise money for the fund. An annual telethon is one among several special events that use volunteers. Interview.

6

Families

Perhaps Murphy Brown put it best in her response to former vice president Dan Quayle: "Families come in all shapes and sizes."

Often families need help from outside sources and institutions to stay together or be brought together. As a volunteer you can help individuals to a better family experience. If you're people-oriented and care about the state of the American family today, you can help.

Listings

CATHOLIC GUARDIAN SOCIETY OF BROOKLYN AND QUEENS
191 Joralemon St.
Brooklyn, NY 11201
Contact: Volunteer Coordinator
(718) 330-0698

The society provides a number of educational and recreational programs for teens and families, including foster care and adoption services. Volunteers work one evening a week or on weekends planning special events, running recreational activities for the disabled, tutoring children ranging from grade-school level through high school, acting as foster grandparents or simply as buddies taking children to museums, parks, or movies. Applicants should, obviously, work well with children. Interview, references, state child abuse clearance, three-hour orientation.

COURT APPOINTED SPECIAL ADVOCATES
350 Broadway
Suite 1107
New York, NY 10013
Contact: Muriel Leconte, Volunteer Program Coordinator
(212) 334-4010
CASA is a nonprofit organization that uses both professional staff and volunteers to assist children in New York's troubled foster care program. Since 1979, CASA has been dedicated to providing a more meaningful judicial review for foster care children seeking permanent family living situations. New York City CASA is one of 500 CASA programs nationwide. Volunteers monitor the cases of over 1,000 children a year. It's a rewarding way to help kids who have fallen between the cracks of our complex judicial system. Interview, extensive orientation, training, in-service seminars.

EXPANDING OPTIONS FOR TEEN MOTHERS
250 Jay St.
Brooklyn, NY 11201
Contact: Sybil Tabuteau
(718) 260-5730
Young mothers can certainly use your volunteer help adjusting to parenthood while still maturing themselves. Expanding Options provides various educational opportunities to teen mothers. Programs run through the school year and need tutors in math, reading, writing, and other basic skills. A four-hour weekly commitment is asked. Interview, references.

HEARTSEASE HOME
216 E. 70th St.
New York, NY 10021
Contact: Gerald Keener, Executive Director
(212) 249-3107

This is a home for teenage girls in New York's foster care system who are preparing for independent living. The volunteer opportunities are primarily clerical in nature, from stuffing envelopes to word processing. Obviously office or computer skills are a plus. Interview, orientation.

HOMES FOR THE HOMELESS
36 Cooper Square
New York, NY 10003
Contact: Kathy Kniep, Educational Programs Coordinator
(212) 529-5252

Homes for the Homeless has four New York City residences that provide transitional housing and other assistance to homeless families. In nearly a decade they have helped over 6,000 such families in need, with help from volunteers. The programs focus on all members of the family, featuring Jump Start Educational programs for children as well as after-school learning programs. There are programs to help adolescents and to assist and educate parents. Résumé, interview, references.

See also chapter 8, "Homeless."

INWOOD HOUSE
320 E. 82nd St.
New York, NY 10028
Contact: Clare Reilly
(212) 861-4400

Inwood House provides assistance to pregnant and parenting teenagers. The organization has two locations, in Manhattan at the address listed above, and in the Bronx on 167th Street and Prospect Avenue. Volunteer services include providing child care on site, answering phones at the maternity residence, working in the library, and providing recreational activities for teens. If you would like to teach teenage girls

Families

dance, makeup application, cooking, or other skills, this is a marvelous opportunity. Interview, references.

JEWISH BOARD OF FAMILY AND CHILDREN'S SERVICES
Mary S. Froelich Division of Volunteer Services
120 W. 57th St.
New York, NY 10019
Contact: Volunteer Division
(212) 397-4090

Volunteer opportunities to help families are available at a host of locations throughout the city, working in conjunction with this major umbrella agency.

Opportunities you might consider include the board's Jewish Big Brother and Big Sister program, camp program, Family Location Service, holiday toy program, and Telephone Language Companion program, along with outreach and other special assignments working with children. There are other programs, as well. The board works to meet the needs of people in crisis through mental health and social services. Interview, three references, training where necessary.

See also chapter 14, "Umbrella Organizations and Referral Groups."

KOREAN SERVICES FAMILY CENTER
P.O. Box 20202
New York, NY 10001
Contact: Ji Young Kim, Executive Director
(212) 465-0664

The center serves family members of all ages, focusing primarily on domestic violence and dealing with family crises. There is a need for interpreters as well as administrative support and help with fund-raising. If you speak fluent English and Korean, you can help clients going to court, dealing with administrative or housing issues, and in many other contexts.

LEFFERTS HOMESTEAD CHILDREN'S HISTORIC HOUSE
Prospect Park
Flatbush Ave. and Empire Blvd.
Brooklyn, NY 11225
Contact: Prospect Park Volunteer Office
(718) 965-8960
Lefferts Homestead Children's Historic House
(718) 965-6505

Besides a wealth of horticultural opportunities, the park also has a family volunteer program. Parents and children (seven and older) may volunteer together to help younger children participate in games and activities in the Lefferts Homestead Children's Museum. The museum offers a variety of 19th-century fun and games for children of all ages, and family volunteering is a special part of what volunteering is all about—togetherness. Classes can also volunteer through special park programs.

See also chapter 2, "Zoos, Parks, and Other Outdoor Opportunities" and chapter 6, "Families."

PLANNED PARENTHOOD
810 Seventh Ave.
New York, NY 10019
Contact: Cassandra Dancy
(212) 541-7800

Billed as "America's most trusted name in women's health," Planned Parenthood is a nationwide organization focusing on issues of reproductive and contraceptive health. The New York office uses volunteers in various departments including the media, public relations, public affairs, human resources, library, development, marketing, and others. If you're interested in being involved in areas such as family planning and prenatal care you may want to help Planned Parenthood. Interview.

Families

SOCIETY FOR SEAMEN'S CHILDREN
25 Hyatt St.
Staten Island, NY 10301
Contact: Mary Thompson, Development Director
(718) 447-7740

The society is dedicated to helping families through counseling. Volunteers help out with clerical work or by taking care of the children of family members who are in group sessions. Must either have good office skills (including data entry experience) or work well with children. Interview.

SUPPORTIVE CHILDREN'S ADVOCACY NETWORK (SCAN)
207 E. 27th St.
New York, NY 10016
Contact: Volunteer Coordinator
(212) 683-2695

SCAN's mission is to alleviate child neglect and abuse. It works with the entire family, in the community, offering school recreation and socialization groups, tutoring, cultural and creative-arts programs, and a comprehensive summer program. Bronx SCAN includes a youth leadership council, summer day camp, an adolescent-service unit, and much more. The Family Renewal Center offers a long list of programs to assist families affected by parents' substance abuse, while the Overman Children and Families Therapeutic Center completes SCAN's holistic, family-focused network. Volunteers can help out in most of these programs, often working directly with one family. Interview, references, training, supervision.

7
Community

In a city as big as New York, communities come in all shapes, sizes, and configurations. Community centers, Y's, and neighborhood associations provide activities ranging from sports to arts and crafts for everyone from toddlers to seniors. Volunteering provides a great way to hone your own skills while teaching others. One of the nicest aspects of community volunteering is that it's usually in a familiar locale, which takes away the pressures of commuting, finding a strange address, traveling long distances after dark, and so on.

So, Why Volunteer in the Community?

If you've ever strolled past youngsters at play in abandoned buildings, teens hanging out in bleak alleyways, seniors sitting day after day on the same park benches, and homeless people curling up for the night on a neighborhood stoop, you might consider helping provide the members of (whatever you consider) your community a better way of life. Community volunteering is a wonderful way to feel connected to the neighborhood and/or your ethnic culture.

It's also a great way to meet people. Many such volunteers have been known to make friends in the neighborhood. Others find that they can actually improve the quality of life around them by raising high school reading scores, advocating for a much-needed stop light, or just serving a homeless family a hot meal. One basketball coach at a New York City Y explained his reason for coaching a dozen teenage boys: "I get to be Pat Riley for a little while twice a week. . . . I love it!" Let's not underestimate the power of ego gratification.

Community centers, Y's, neighborhood associations, and settlement houses are all multiservice facilities, with neighborhood associations and settlement houses generally offering additional social programs, such as shelters or soup kitchens for the homeless and AIDS-related services. But if you want to work with the city's youth, all the kinds of groups mentioned are great places to teach, tutor, coach, mentor, and, most important, provide a positive role model.

Community Boards

There are 59 community boards in the five boroughs involved with governing the city at a local level. They deal with everything from deciding whether to allow a restaurant to expand into a sidewalk café, to putting up a much needed stoplight, to allowing (or not allowing) a real estate mogul to replace a local playground with his or her latest 50-story skyscraper.

While board members are volunteers (with a lot of time to give) selected by the borough president's office and the City Council members, you can also get involved. As a member of the public you can voice your views on issues of concern or perhaps lend your expertise in a particular area when needed.

Community boards can also be of service to those looking to volunteer in their neighborhood. The boards have extensive mailing lists and are generally familiar with groups and organizations in their area. For a complete list of community boards in the five boroughs, or to find the community board nearest you, call the Office of the Mayor, Community Assistance Bureau: (212) 788-7418.

Another source that you might contact for information on neighborhood houses in your community is:

United Neighborhood Houses,
   New York
475 Park Ave. South
New York, NY 10016
(212) 481-5570

Some Community Listings

The list below suggests some community-based organizations in which you can participate. There may be more just around the corner from you.

BIG APPLE GREETER
1 Centre St.
New York, NY 10007
Contact: Wendy Pedhowitz, Director of Volunteers
(212) 669-2364
This is a unique opportunity to enrich the New York experience for some of our many visitors. As a volunteer you will be paired with a tourist and will accompany them through favorite parts of your own neighborhood or others that you're familiar with. You will also visit specialty shops, cultural attractions, historic buildings, and the places that make New York a one-of-a-kind city. Greeters will be trained in putting together a flexible itinerary. You need only be 18 or over, available for two four-hour visits per month, pleasant, courteous, and ready to show an out-of-town visitor a good time in the Big Apple. Interview, training.

Community

BROOKLYN CENTER FOR THE PERFORMING ARTS AT BROOKLYN COLLEGE
P.O. Box 100163
Brooklyn, NY 11210
Contact: Reva Cooper, Director of Marketing and Communications
(718) 951-5006

The center primarily utilizes volunteers for community outreach programs, hence its listing under "Community." You can help throughout Brooklyn, at street fairs and other community-related projects. Outreach projects also include phone calls and mailings to various community organizations. Interview.

CHINATOWN MANPOWER PROJECT
70 Mulberry St.
New York, NY 10013
Contact: Cambao De Duong, Deputy Director
(212) 571-1696

Can you help immigrants speak and converse in English? This is a chance to try your skills with new Asian immigrants and refugees. Bilingual skills a plus, but other volunteer opportunities are available in job development, cultivating potential employers and on the organization's advisory committee. Résumé, interview.

EDUCATIONAL ALLIANCE
197 E. Broadway
New York, NY 10002
Contact: Suzanne Maltz, Director of Development
(212) 475-6200, ext. 373

Started well over 100 years ago on the Lower East Side of Manhattan, this multipurpose agency today provides educational and recreational activities for all ages. Now, with 19 locations—mostly in lower Manhattan—they provide services from the cradle to the grave. Volunteer opportunities include Head Start, day care nursery school, lunch programs, tutoring, clerical duties, seminars, and cultural and recreational classes for seniors. Interview; for child care, state child abuse clearance.

HIGHBRIDGE COMMUNITY LIFE CENTER
979 Ogden Ave.
Bronx, NY 10452
Contact: Karen Gioscia, Director of Volunteers
(718) 681-2222

Serving the Highbridge neighborhood, the center offers children and adults recreational activities, classes, counseling, and health screenings. You can assist as a tutor, helping students learn to speak English, or in other areas. Friendly visiting with seniors and an AIDS outreach program also lend support to members of the community. Interview, references.

JEWISH COMMUNITY CENTER OF STATEN ISLAND
475 Victory Blvd.
Staten Island, NY 10301
Contact: Evelyn Barren, Director of Adult Services
(718) 981-1500

The center has two branches, one on the north shore and one on the south shore. They offer opportunities ranging from clerical work to assisting in a classroom. Computer mavens can provide much-appreciated help in the tremendous computer program, while those interested in working with teens and youths can coach or teach recreational activities. There is also an English-as-a-second-language program, taught by volunteers, and a large senior center. Interview, screening, possible medical screening.

THE JEWISH COMMUNITY CENTER ON THE UPPER WEST SIDE
180 W. 80th St.
New York, NY 10024
Contact: Susan Zuckerman, Associate Director
(212) 580-0099

An important part of the JCC's role in the community is referring volunteers to agencies around New York City. The JCC works with numerous agencies around the five boroughs, including:

Community

ANSCHE CHESED MEN'S SHELTER
B'NAI JESHURUN SOUP KITCHEN AND HOMELESS SHELTER
JEWISH BOARD OF FAMILY AND CHILDREN'S SERVICES BIG BROTHER/BIG SISTER PROGRAM
THE DOME PROJECT

This particular JCC looks to meet the needs of the community with social, cultural, and educational programs. The center offers neighborhood youngsters various opportunities, from preschool programs to after-school recreational activities. There are also activities and groups for adults, including single parents and seniors. Volunteers are matched with the program that suits their interests, such as Sukkah decorating at local hospitals or working with new readers in the Gift of Literacy program. Interview.

See also chapter 14, "Umbrella Organizations and Referral Groups."

JEWISH COMMUNITY HOUSE OF BENSONHURST
7802 Bay Pkwy.
Brooklyn, NY 11214
Contact: Richard Smuckler, Assistant Director
(718) 331-6800

Nearly 70 years old, this agency provides social services and recreational activities. It operates as a community center; membership programs range from nursery school to senior services. Because of the huge number of Russian immigrants in the area, the center has a major service center for them. Volunteers can help in the nursery school program or the after-school program, assist with one-to-one tutoring for children or adults, work on activities with seniors, and more. Interview, references, orientation.

JOINT ACTION IN COMMUNITY SERVICE
Office of Job Corps
201 Varick St.
New York, NY 10014
Contact: Judy Conway, Regional Director
(212) 337-2287

Joint Action in Community Service and the Job Corps are

approximately 30 years old. Interested volunteers act as advisers to young men looking to set their goals and ready themselves for their future in the workplace. You will, by telephone, assess the needs of the young men involved in the program and provide them information, referrals, advice, and support. There is a lot of flexibility in terms of hours and location. If you're over 18 and interested in helping disadvantaged youths become a self-sufficient and productive part of society, this is a solid way to help. Interview; training will be provided.

KINGSBRIDGE HEIGHTS COMMUNITY CENTER
3101 Kingsbridge Terrace
Brooklyn, NY 10463
Contact: Lori Spector, Associate Executive Director
A settlement house, this multipurpose center has programs for the disabled as well as for teens and seniors. Its Thanksgiving dinner requires numerous volunteers. If you're looking to help on a weekly basis, you might work as a child-care assistant, in the Head Start learning program, or in the office, on the switchboard or at the computer terminals. Volunteers are screened, depending on the program they're interested in. Interview, orientation.

KIPS BAY BOYS AND GIRLS CLUB
1930 Randall Ave.
Bronx, NY 10473
Contact: Dale Drake, Associate Director
(718) 893-8254
This is an opportunity to help the neighborhood's youth through recreational activities. If you're good with youngsters from six to sixteen years old, you may find a rewarding opportunity coaching a team, tutoring children, helping students with their homework, or lending supervisory support in the game room. Applicants must submit a résumé and cover letter. Interview, on-site training.

See also chapter 3, "Children."

Community

LENOX HILL NEIGHBORHOOD ASSOCIATION
331 E. 70th St.
New York, NY 10021
Contact: Ellen Block
(212) 744-5022

For over 100 years, the Lenox Hill Neighborhood Association, a settlement house, has been serving the Upper East Side of Manhattan. There are a lot of ways in which you can help them better serve some 20,000 people each year. The Head Start program, for three- to five-year-olds, uses volunteers to assist teachers in classrooms. After-school programs provide tutors and volunteers to lead recreational activities. Teen programs use professionals as speakers on career nights as well as assistants and coaches in recreational programs. There are also adult programs, including fitness groups and English-as-a-second-language classes. The senior center also uses many volunteers. Other programs include community advocacy, homeless outreach, an overnight shelter, rehabilitation, and holiday programs. Interview, references, orientation.

LINCOLN SQUARE NEIGHBORHOOD CENTER
250 W. 65th St.
New York, NY 10023
Contact: Walter Edge, Executive Director
(212) 874-0860

This settlement house near Lincoln Square offers a wide range of options for those interested in giving a few hours a week. Mentor programs and after-school programs have you helping neighborhood youngsters with school subjects and classes in crafts, painting, dance, and other areas in the arts. Assisting in Friday night basketball tournaments for teens is a great way to have some fun while volunteering. The group also has a senior program. Résumé, interview, references; medical requirements for working with children.

MOSHOLU MONTEFIORE COMMUNITY CENTER
3450 DeKalb Ave.
Bronx, NY 10467
Contact: Bob Altman, Assistant Executive Director
(718) 882-4000

Here's an opportunity to help from the classroom to the kitchen to the coaching box.

This 40 + -year-old, multipurpose north Bronx facility sees over 2,000 people pass through its doors on any given day. The center has child day care, an after-school program, an immigration program, and a senior center and offers a number of classes and workshops. A fun way to help on weekends is to get involved as a coach in the baseball league, which has some 750 kids participating. Volunteers must have no criminal record. Interview, references, training.

NATIONAL COUNCIL OF JEWISH WOMEN
9 E. 69th St.
New York, NY 10021
Contact: Volunteer Department
(212) 535-5900

The council provides community services for all ages, races, and religious backgrounds. They work on improving life primarily in the areas of aging, children and youth, constitutional rights, women's rights, Jewish life, and issues relating to Israel. Volunteers are needed in the Pantry Program to assist in taking in and packaging food. The council operates a thrift shop on Ninth Avenue in Manhattan and also acts as a referral service for volunteers, hooking them up with other sites around the city. You should be a high school graduate and make a three-hour minimum weekly commitment. Interviews.

RETIRED SENIOR VOLUNTEER PROGRAM (RSVP)
Part of Community Services Society
Main Office
105 E. 22nd St.
New York, NY 10010
(212) 254-8900

Community

If you're retired and over 55, you too can give a few hours a week of community service through the largest senior volunteer program in the city. Part of a national program, RSVP can place you in a volunteer position in practically any part of the five boroughs. The program offers a wide range of services, from tutoring in the schools to planting in the botanical gardens, to helping other seniors with their taxes.

See also chapter 14, "Umbrella Organizations and Referral Groups."

RIVERDALE COMMUNITY CENTER
660 W. 237th St.
Bronx, NY 10463
Contact: Ferne LaDue, Executive Director
(718) 796-4724

Providing a wide range of activities and educational opportunities, the center focuses 'on social guidance for neighborhood youngsters and teens. If you have a flair for theatrics you might help out in the teen theater by playing piano, making costumes, or helping rehearsals run smoothly. Tutors are also an important part of the center. The center, which operates out of a school, emphasizes short-term volunteer needs for specific projects. Long-term volunteers are welcome, but only if they can commit to at least the full nine- or 10-month semester. Interview, screening.

SENECA CENTER
1241 Lafayette Ave.
Bronx, NY 10474
Contact: R. Edward Lee, Executive Director
(718) 378-1300

If you're near the Hunts Point Peninsula in the Bronx, here's a chance to make a difference for the youth of the neighborhood.

The center's purpose is to provide educational and recreational opportunities to neighborhood youths. Volunteers act as group leaders for various activities and tutor youngsters in various school subjects. Interview.

UNIVERSITY SETTLEMENT SOCIETY OF NEW YORK
114 Eldridge St.
New York, NY 10002
Contact: Gerard Duphiney, Director of Youth Services
(212) 674-9120

The society has 15 programs, all open to you as a volunteer. Services in this 90-year-old facility include literacy classes for adults, Meals on Wheels, and social and educational programs serving the Lower East Side. The youth program offers evening tutoring once a week between 6 P.M. and 7:30 P.M.; and after-school groups meet from 3 P.M. to 6 P.M. Volunteers are asked to commit to one day a week, and consistency is important. There is also a Foster Grandparents program. Interview, screening.

YMCA
Main Office
333 Seventh Ave.
New York, NY 10001
Contact: Ellie Murphy
(212) 630-9600

The YMCA has been a significant part of New York City since 1852. Branches in all five boroughs serve men and women of all ages. Volunteers form an integral part of the organization, and you can join in. Y programs include teen development, child development, camping, health enhancements, community development, and much more.

If you get involved, you'll be one of approximately 4,000 volunteers who work in several programs. Policy volunteers take an active role in decision making and the orchestration of plans and procedures to enhance Y programs. Other volunteers help in fund-raising, after-school programs, fitness, or membership. Individuals such as lawyers or architects are considered "resource volunteers" and are called upon for guidance and advice in various areas. Volunteer opportunities also exist for groups affiliated with corporations. Such volunteer groups often help with holiday celebrations, street fairs, and open houses. After calling the Main Y you'll be referred to the Y nearest you. Interview.

Community

There are 19 branches, providing over 100 programs in nearly 2 million square feet of space. Each Y has a character of its own and serves a distinct section of the city.

BEDFORD Y
1121 Bedford Ave.
Brooklyn, NY 11216

BROOKLYN CENTRAL Y
218 Hicks St.
Brooklyn, NY 11201

CENTRAL QUEENS Y
89-25 Parsons Blvd.
Jamaica, NY 11432

BRONX Y
2244 Westchester Ave.
Bronx, NY 10462

CHINATOWN Y
100 Hester St.
New York, NY 10002

CROSS ISLAND Y
238-10 Hillside Ave.
Queens, NY 11426

FLATBUSH Y
1401 Flatbush Ave.
Brooklyn, NY 11210

FLUSHING Y
138-46 Northern Blvd.
Flushing, NY 11354

GREENPOINT Y
99 Meserole Ave.
Brooklyn, NY 11222

HARLEM Y
180 W. 135th St.
New York, NY 10030

INTERNATIONAL Y
71 W. 23rd St.
Suite 1904
New York, NY 10010

LONG ISLAND CITY Y
27-04 41st Ave.
Long Island City, NY 11101

NORTH BROOKLYN Y
Eastern District
125 Humboldt St.
Brooklyn, NY 11203

PROSPECT PARK Y
357 Ninth St.
Brooklyn, NY 11215

STATEN ISLAND Y
651 Broadway
Staten Island, NY 10310

VANDERBILT Y
224 E. 47th St.
New York, NY 10017

WESTSIDE Y
5 W. 63rd St.
New York, NY 10023

YOUNG MEN'S HEBREW ASSOCIATION/YOUNG WOMEN'S HEBREW ASSOCIATION

New York City's YM/YWHA's offer a variety of programs, including special events, concerts, lectures, preschool activities, and recreational activities for youths, adults, and seniors. They provide cultural, performing arts and other programs in their respective neighborhoods. Volunteer opportunities vary from one Y to the next. Since the YM/YWHA's are independently run, the best way to find out what any one in particular is looking for is to contact it. Some have many opportunities, while others keep a list of volunteers on hand primarily for special events, fund-raising activities, and special mailings. Training and screening will depend on the position applied for.

SAMUEL FIELD/BAY TERRACE YM/YWHA
58-20 Little Neck Pkwy.
Little Neck, NY 11362
Contact: Sue Nathanson, Director of Special Projects
(718) 225-6750

One of the many multifaceted YM/YWHA's offering programs for all ages. Has an enormous senior center, from which it draws many of its volunteers (see Seniors, "Seniors Helping Seniors"). At the other end of the age spectrum are a nursery school and child care program, which together have about 200 youngsters involved. If you're looking for a few valuable community hours of volunteering per week you might assist in the many classes offered at the Ys. Also, if you have special skills that translate well to youngsters, you might teach in the after-school programs. For example, a former Ping-Pong champion offers a couple of hours two afternoons a week to teach the game to youngsters. Interview, references, screening.

Some of New York's other YM/YWHA's operating independently include:

BOROUGH PARK YM/YWHA
4912 14th Ave.
Brooklyn, NY 11219
(718) 438-5921

CENTRAL QUEENS YM/YWHA
67-09 108th St.
Forest Hills, NY 11375
(718) 268-5011

KINGS BAY YM/YWHA
3495 Nostrand Ave.
Brooklyn, NY 11236

THE 92nd STREET YM/YWHA
1395 Lexington Ave.
New York, NY 10128
(212) 415-5470

RIVERDALE YM/YWHA
5625 Arlington Ave.
Bronx, NY 10471
(718) 548-8200

**YM/YWHA OF WASHINGTON
HEIGHTS AND INWOOD**
54 Nagle Ave.
New York, NY 10040
(212) 569-6200

8

Homeless

"The key to helping the homeless population is trying to accept them as you would accept any other population," says Ellen Block of the Lenox Hill Neighborhood Association.

One sad reality of our times is that for many, many reasons New York City has a large homeless population. We can hope an answer to the problem of homelessness will be found, but in the meantime all we can do is try and assist these people in whatever small ways we can.

Most homeless individuals are on the streets because they can't manage in the mainstream. The reasons vary; some people are addicted to drugs or alcohol; others suffer from mental illnesses or physical disabilities; still others have lost their jobs and subsequently their homes. Some are quite alone, while others have either abandoned their families or been abandoned by them. If you work with the homeless, you must set your goals at a realistic level. There is no easy solution, but you can lend a hand toward improving their situation.

Tips on Working with the Homeless Population

▼ *Don't ask too many questions.* If they want to talk to you (once they feel comfortable with you) they will—if not, so be it. If people do open up to you, be a good listener and don't find fault with their stories or be argumentative.

▼ *Build trust.* In many ways, making a connection with an individual can be much more effective than serving a meal. If you can build their trust, often you can make more of a difference.

▼ *Don't try to force your ideas onto someone else.* Provide possible alternatives, not definite answers.

▼ *Show empathy, not pity.*

▼ *Respect the right to privacy.* Homeless people have little privacy and few possessions. Be cautious and respectful of their space and their things.

▼ *Be supportive.* This is a population that has been ignored and neglected by too many people. You must be accepting and patient while not being judgmental or condescending. Effective volunteers take the time to really think about the plight of the people with whom they're working.

In fairness to yourself and to the people with whom you will be interacting, if you are uncomfortable around or frightened by homeless people or don't feel that you can interact on a nonjudgmental basis, these are not the volunteer opportunities for you. That doesn't mean you're a bad person, it simply means your goals and objectives for volunteering ought to be directed elsewhere.

For information on shelters in various locations throughout the city, including churches and synagogues, you might call the Partnership for the Homeless at (212) 684-3444.

Listings

BROTHERHOOD SOUP KITCHEN AND PANTRY
Brotherhood Baptist Church
232 St. Marks Ave.
Brooklyn, NY 11238
Contact: Ms. Palmer Tuesday–Friday, 3 P.M.–6 P.M.
(718) 638-7763, ext. 10

This community-based Brooklyn soup kitchen is on the border of Crown Heights and Park Slope. Between 11 A.M. and 2 P.M. Tuesday–Friday, their kitchen serves nearly 100 lunches a day. You can help them by serving food, washing dishes, cleaning up and assisting with other related duties. Volunteers are asked to participate for one full three-hour weekly shift. Interview.

CITY HARVEST
159 W. 25th St.
New York, NY 10001
Contact: Maria Pitullo, Volunteer Coordinator
(212) 463-0456

This special service picks up surplus food and distributes it to soup kitchens, pantries, and shelters throughout New York City. You can help here in the development department, with mailings, organizing canned-food drives, and so on. You can also serve as an agency liaison—finding sites, conducting surveys, and helping City Harvest with its special mission to provide food for the homeless. Interview.

CHURCH OF THE HOLY TRINITY
316 E. 88th St.
New York, NY 10128
Contact: Parish Secretary
(212) 289-4100

The Holy Trinity Neighborhood Center provides a Saturday afternoon soup kitchen, a luncheon program for seniors, a homeless shelter, and an AIDS support residence and ministry. Volunteers help by serving food and providing support

Homeless

to the elderly, to people with HIV/AIDS, and to the homeless. There is also an on-premises thrift shop where volunteers
assist in providing clothing to the center's guests.

COALITION FOR THE HOMELESS
89 Chambers St.
Third Floor
New York, NY 10007
Contact: Michael Polenberg
(212) 964-5900

The coalition provides advocacy and services to New York's
homeless population. The Grand Central Food Program, in
particular, needs volunteers to hand out meals. Volunteers
also refer homeless people to shelters, to possible jobs, and
so on. The coalition asks that you commit one hour a week
between 7 P.M. and 9 P.M. to helping. Interview.

COMMUNITY PROJECTS AND PROGRAMS
25 W. 132nd St.
Suite 8-L
New York, NY 10037
Contact: Sheard Wright, Executive Director
(212) 926-5530

CPAP offers various programs to assist the less fortunate improve their employment status and find other human services
they may need. CPAP not only recruits volunteers for its own
facility but also refers help to other agencies. Volunteers in
CPAP work to develop activities, help with office and administrative work, and assist the program coordinators. Interview.

GRAND CENTRAL PARTNERSHIP MULTISERVICE CENTER
152 E. 44th St.
New York, NY 10017
Contact: Tayhilia Fuller Bey
(212) 818-1220, ext. 16

The center features a clothing bank for the homeless and uses
volunteers to operate the clothing room, maintain order, sort
garments, and supervise clients. It's an ideal opportunity for
volunteers who work nine to five: the operating hours are
Monday through Friday from 6 to 8 P.M. Kitchen help is also
needed for the center's Self-Help Program's food services.

HOLY APOSTLES SOUP KITCHEN
296 Ninth Ave.
New York, NY 10001
Contact: Stacy Allen
(212) 924-0167

This is an opportunity to directly feed New York's homeless and hungry. Volunteers greet guests who need to see a counselor. Distributing tickets, maintaining order, and serving food are the responsibilities involved in working in the soup kitchen. The hours of operation are 9 A.M. to 1 P.M. Monday–Friday.

HOMES FOR THE HOMELESS
36 Cooper Sq.
New York, NY 10003
Contact: Kathy Kniep, Educational Programs Coordinator
(212) 529-5252

The largest provider of transitional housing and services for homeless families in New York City, Homes for the Homeless has four family locations in New York City, all of which use volunteers to help educate children and adults in a number of areas. You can also help in workshops and with special outings. Résumé, two references, interview.

HOUSING WORKS
594 Broadway
Suite 700
New York, NY 10012
Contact: Brigid Lang, Volunteer Coordinator
(212) 966-0466

Since 1991, Housing Works has provided safe, permanent housing for over 500 men, women, and children with HIV/AIDS. Working in one of its thrift shops may provide a gentle introduction to working with the AIDS community. There are also job training programs, the Hospital Visiting Program, and a theater project, which stages plays for the public. There is also a need for people to participate in advocacy and public policy, helping clients receive proper legal and entitlement services. Special events, mailings, and administrative support are also areas to consider. Interview, references, training, orientation.

Homeless

See also chapter 12, "Health and Human Services" for other HIV/AIDS-related programs.

HUNGER ACTION NETWORK OF NEW YORK STATE
115 E. 23rd St.
New York, NY 10010
Contact: Paul Getsos
(212) 505-2055

A statewide antihunger, antipoverty organization, HANNY is working to change the long-term problems of hunger through public education and legislative advocacy. There are a number of ways to get involved, including work in the various centers (for example, in the kitchens) and in the offices. HANNY also has a food stamp outreach program that uses volunteers. There are programs for public speaking and mentors who work with the homeless. Interview, training.

PROJECT HOSPITALITY
530 Bay St.
Staten Island, NY 10304
Contact: Paulette Williams or Harry Muselman,
  Volunteer Coordinators
(718) 448-1544

This is one of the leading agencies assisting the poor and homeless people of Staten Island. Volunteer opportunities include helping at the soup kitchen preparing or serving meals (Tuesdays and Thursdays from one to three), helping in the administrative offices, answering phones, coordinating fundraising events, staying overnight in the shelter, helping tutor children, and following up on families who have been placed in permanent housing. After an interview you will have to provide two personal references. Special training for certain areas is provided.

PROJECT RETURN FOUNDATION
10 Astor Place
New York, NY 10003
Contact: Roger Faison
(212) 979-8800

For over 20 years, this busy agency has been helping people in various communities throughout Manhattan, the Bronx, and Brooklyn with drug treatment programs, battered children's groups, a parole transition project and many other services. Volunteers assist counselors with groups and help in the office with clerical duties. Interview, orientation.

ST. FRANCIS XAVIER CHURCH
55 W. 15th St.
New York, NY 10011
Contact: John Bucki or Ann Cleary
(212) 627-2100
The church operates a Sunday soup kitchen that serves over 1,000 meals every week as well as offering other assistance to homeless families. Between 8:30 A.M. and 3:30 P.M. on Sundays, volunteers are needed to prepare food, set tables, serve food, and clean and wash up.

ST. IGNATIUS LOYOLA CHURCH
980 Park Ave.
New York, NY 10028
Contact: Miriam S. Klinger
(212) 288-3588
One of several churches affiliated with the St. Vincent de Paul Society, St. Ignatius Loyola provides an outreach program including friendly visits to the large senior population on Manhattan's Upper East Side. It also has a shelter for the homeless, works with children, and hosts day events and theme parties at the church. Interview; training where necessary.

STEPS
320 E. 96th St.
New York, NY 10128
Contact: Gaila Coughlin, Deputy Director
(212) 410-4891
Can you teach job skills?

At STEPS you can tutor welfare mothers in the skills they need to get jobs, and assist in educating the homeless to help themselves develop basic job skills. STEPS also utilizes volunteers to help teachers keep records and to research possible fund-raising opportunities. They also have a summer youth program that'll put you back in a fun summer-camp-like environment. Interview and training.

WEST END INTERGENERATIONAL RESIDENCE
483 West End Ave.
New York, NY 10024
Contact: Erika Silverstein, Coordinator of Volunteer Services
(212) 873-6300, ext. 321

This unique residence provides housing and educational and social services for homeless seniors, mothers, and children. A 12-story facility, the Intergenerational Residence has over 80 transitional housing units. Three generations reside together and participate in various activities. Career guidance, parenting workshops, and independent living skills are taught as part of the program. Volunteers help provide child care, lead programs and workshops, assist with special events and fundraising, provide friendly visiting, and more. The group asks for at least a two-hour-a-week, three-month commitment. Interview, references; medical requirements including TB test, state child abuse clearance.

YORKVILLE COMMON PANTRY
8 E. 109th St.
New York, NY 10029
Contact: Sheila Coralles
(212) 410-2264

Since 1980 the Common Pantry has been serving food to the neighborhood's homeless on various schedules. They operate from two locations on 91st Street and First Avenue and at the 109th Street main location. Volunteers need only have the willingness and sensitivity to deal with the homeless population.

9

Libraries

Besides not talking too loudly on the premises, library volunteers should be familiar with the library's workings and appreciate its significance in the community. This is a marvelous opportunity for book lovers.

Neighborhood libraries throughout the five boroughs are part of three main library systems: the Brooklyn Public Library; the New York Public Library, which includes Manhattan, Staten Island, and the Bronx; and the Queensborough Library System. The many community-based libraries offer opportunities to volunteer, highlighted by two significant programs, the literacy program (see Education) and the Friends of the Library programs listed below. In addition, there are a few research libraries (including the 42nd Street library), which also have volunteer positions. Involvement in a library can mean anything from working at the information desk to campaigning for more funding. There are special events, fund-raising book sales, and more.

According to Stacy Leigh, Friends of the Library coordinator for the Brooklyn Public Library system, "We have plenty of people who work regular full-time weekday jobs come and volunteer a few hours a week in their local library."

Listings

BROOKLYN PUBLIC LIBRARY
Grand Army Plaza
Brooklyn, NY 11238
Contact: Stacy Leigh, Friends of the Library coordinator, or the local branch librarian
(718) 780-7806

Friends of the Brooklyn Public Library is an integral part of 24 of Brooklyn's 54 branch libraries. And you too can be a Friend.

Friends groups work in four major areas: raising the community's interest in and awareness of the library; promoting the resources, services, and programs provided by the branch libraries; lobbying officials and the government on behalf of the library; and raising funds for materials that would enhance the local library. As a Friend you would participate in everything from letter-writing campaigns to book and bake sales to helping organize the annual walkathon. Contact either the central branch in Brooklyn at Grand Army Plaza or your local branch. Interview, orientation.

NEW YORK PUBLIC LIBRARY
Central Research Library
Fifth Ave. and 42nd St.
Volunteer Office
Room M6
New York, NY 10018
Contact: Volunteer Office
(212) 930-0501

Don't be intimidated by the lions in front; this huge library is indeed a friendly place for volunteers—some 300 to be exact—and you too can participate. Volunteers work at information desks, help with mailings, teach English as a second language, act as docents, and much more. Résumé, interview, training where applicable.

NEW YORK PUBLIC LIBRARY FOR THE PERFORMING ARTS
Lincoln Center
Contact: Marcia Loyd, Volunteer Coordinator
(212) 870-1605
For anyone interested in the arts, this is an opportunity to work with a marvelous collection of theater- and film-related books and more. New York's premier arts and entertainment library uses volunteers in several capacities, working at book sales, at the information desk, and at the annual bazaar where videos, books, photos, and collectibles are sorted, labeled, priced, and sold to the public. Interview, training.

QUEENS BOROUGH PUBLIC LIBRARY
89-11 Merrick Blvd.
Jamaica, NY 11432
Contact: Ricki Wasserman, Volunteer Coordinator
(718) 990-0872
If you believe in the sanctity of the library and its importance in your community, you might want to volunteer at one of the 62 branch libraries in Queens. Last year, nearly 400 volunteers put in over 20,000 hours in the various programs. Volunteers support library staff by helping with clerical work and library programs. There are opportunities to become involved in reading programs, discussion groups, and story-time programs for kids, or you can help raise funds through book sales. Applicants can contact their branch library or the central library (at the phone number above). Interview, orientation.

SCHOMBURG CENTER FOR RESEARCH IN BLACK CULTURE
515 Malcolm X Blvd.
New York, NY 10037-1801
Contact: Elsie Gibbs, Volunteer Coordinator
(212) 491-2030
The Schomburg Center is a research library that also offers

forums, exhibits, and special events. Volunteers work as docents, giving informal short presentations to the public on the
center's history and its current and future exhibitions. Volunteers are also needed as ushers, clerical assistants, in the gift
shop, as hosts and hostesses for special events, and at the
information desk. Special volunteer activities include participating in trips to other New York museums or points of interest such as the United Nations and planning and taking part
in cultural events. Interview.

10

Politics

Politicians come and go, but volunteers are a constant. If you'd like to throw your hat into the volunteer ring you can do a number of things, including working for your favorite candidate by stuffing envelopes, making phone calls, putting up signs and posters, doing research, or performing any number of other tasks. From working for your local assemblyman or assemblywoman on up, there are ways to assist the person, party, or cause you believe in.

Why Volunteer in the Political Arena?

Essentially political work is a way to enrich and improve the life of your neighborhood, community, city, state, or even nation. It's also a great way to learn more about how the system works—and doesn't work.

Many volunteers find that working with a candidate or for a political cause helps get a cause near and dear to them addressed. It's also a stimulating way to meet people who believe in the same principles and ideals that you believe in—and who are doing something about them.

Listings

Because candidates, politicians, and headquarters change and move often, we provide just a few samples below. For more opportunities you might contact your local community board (see listings in Community section). The boards often need volunteer help. Also, they are a good source of information on local political issues and candidates.

You might also contact your city councilperson's office, the party of your choice, or your state assemblyperson's office. The *Green Book*, the official directory of the City of New York, is an annual directory of elected officials and is available in your library. If you like, you can call the City Council office at City Hall, (212) 788-7100. If you tell them where you're located, they can tell you who your local contacts would be.

ACTION FOR COMMUNITY EMPOWERMENT
126 W. 119th St.
New York, NY 10026
Contact: Nia Mason, Organizer/Assistant Director
(212) 932-3324
A community political organization, this nonpartisan group looks out for the political interests of Central Harlem. Volunteers can get involved in community organizing, canvassing the neighborhood, doing phone work, or helping with mailings. Other volunteers help with the newsletter or do slide presentations.

LEAGUE OF WOMEN VOTERS
817 Broadway
New York, NY 10003
Contact: Amy Beissel
(212) 677-5050

A nonpartisan volunteer organization founded in 1920, the League of Women Voters works to promote political responsibility through the informed and active participation of citizens in government.

You can help with voter registration or provide telephone information about voting procedures in New York. Fund-raising drives also use volunteers to help stuff envelopes, among other tasks. People with a penchant for data entry are welcomed to work on the computers as well. Interview, training.

NEW YORK YOUNG REPUBLICAN CLUB
P.O. Box 650052
Fresh Meadows, NY 11365-0052
Contact: Dr. Thomas Robert Stevens, President
(718) 357-7075

The oldest active Young Republican Club in the nation, dating back to 1911, this has 32 committees on which you can volunteer. Included are the Bush Brigade, a charitable outreach program that works with groups like God's Love We Deliver and City Harvest. There are groups promoting HIV/AIDS education in schools, special events, and fund-raising activities. People are also needed to do research. You might also contact other Republican committees such as the Republican County Committee of New York County or the Metropolitan Republican Club.

Politics

11

Seniors

If you enjoy sharing your talents, reading, teaching crafts, and communicating with people who possess a wealth of lifetime achievements and experiences, you'll enjoy working with seniors.

Opportunities in senior centers, nursing homes, and various senior programs throughout the city include leading recreational groups, assisting in feeding, transporting, and escorting patients or residents, and doing shopping or chores for homebound old people. The most significant activity, however, is called friendly visiting, which encompasses everything from teaching a craft to playing a board game or card game to looking through photo albums or assembling one. Many volunteers spend a few hours a week reading to, listening to, or talking with a senior citizen. The key to all of this is establishing a solid relationship. You need to devote two or three weekly hours to the person's needs, and to put yours aside unless they ask to hear about your life.

Why Volunteer to Work with Seniors?

There are a wide range of reasons why you might choose to work with the senior population, from missing your own grandparents to wanting to gain practical experience for a career in gerontology.

But what is needed from you as an individual?

Rema Sessler of the Isabella Geriatric Center in Manhattan recommends "a sense of tremendous patience, the ability not to be judgmental, understanding the aging process, and being able to accept the range of behaviors which may include a loss of cognitive abilities or pleasantries."

As for the effectiveness of working with seniors, Rema adds that "through recreational activities it can be easier to relate and establish a relationship. The activity may be a game or a focus on making something, or it may be attending a concert together. It may be as simple as doing nails together or as complex as writing poetry. When there's a focus, the visit becomes more meaningful."

Tips for Helping Seniors

▼ *Follow through with your commitments.* A few hours a week is a break from your busy daily routine, but it may be the highlight of someone else's week, so don't let him or her down.

▼ *Encourage independence wherever possible and practical.*

▼ *Accept the mood swings that may accompany the aging process and various common medications.* If you are suddenly the scapegoat for the loneliness a person feels due to his or her own family's inattentiveness, don't take it personally.

▼ *Be a good listener.* That includes hearing the same story you may have heard before (possibly several times!).

▼ *After spending time with a senior, assess in your own mind or take notes regarding anything you find (emotionally or physically) out of the ordinary.* This can be discussed with the case manager.

Seniors Helping Seniors

The Samuel Field/Bay Terrace YM/YWHA in Little Neck, Queens, have nearly 1,000 seniors passing through their doors each week for classes and various activities. According to Sue Nathanson, director of special projects, "A good number of our volunteers come from that group. The senior volunteers play a major role in our organization." Many of the listings in this chapter suggest wonderful ways for seniors to remain active in the community and improve the lives of their peers at the same time.

Some Listings for Working with Seniors

Below are several facilities that provide services to seniors. Some provide for you to visit seniors in their own homes, while others are residences, such as nursing homes or hospices.

The facilities listed below, like most others, will have you fill out an application and come in for an interview. Some will request personal references. By New York State law, a PPD test for tuberculosis is needed if you will be feeding seniors. Many facilities will require a medical reference as well. These requirements vary depending on the facility and the task at hand.

BETHLEHEM LUTHERAN CHURCH
6935 Fourth Ave.
Brooklyn, NY 11209
Contact: Cheryl Lynn Heiberg, Executive Director
(718) 748-0650
The church is home to the Bay Ridge Nutrition and Home Care center, offering over 100 meals to homebound elderly people as well as another 100+ meals to senior members of the congregation. As a volunteer you can give a few hours

helping in the kitchen, preparing and serving meals, or distributing lunches to homebound elderly people and the homeless. Clerical help is also needed. Applicants are asked to fill out a questionnaire to match their interests to available opportunities. Interview; training where necessary.

BIALYSTOKER NURSING HOME
228 E. Broadway
New York, NY 10002
Contact: Lauren Weinstein
(212) 475-7755, ext. 48

This Lower East Side Manhattan nursing home has opportunities to assist the elderly by helping them write letters, by reading to them, or with various other one-on-one activities, as well as by providing companionship. Also, if you play a musical instrument or can provide some pleasant form of entertainment you can help brighten the spirits of the residents. Interview, medical requirements, training.

BRONX HOUSE JEWISH COMMUNITY CENTER
990 Pelham Parkway South
Bronx, NY 10461
Contact: Mil Rabinowitz, Supervisor of Older Adults
(718) 792-1800

This Pelham Parkway community center is another example of an agency with various programs including an extensive senior center. Volunteers work as teachers or lecturers. If you are knowledgeable in subjects such as Jewish history, art, or music you might choose to take your skills into this learning environment. Entertainers are also welcome. Interview.

BROOKDALE CENTER ON THE AGING
425 E. 25th St.
New York, NY 10010
Contact: Adele Goldberg
(212) 481-5050

Brookdale has group activities and a respite program for caretakers of people with Alzheimer's disease which provides socialization for people with Alzheimer's. Volunteers help caregivers serve snacks and facilitate recreational activities such as dancing, singing, and various crafts. Applicants are asked for a four-hour weekly commitment. It's important to have some knowledge of what Alzheimer's is all about. Interview, references.

CARING COMMUNITY VOLUNTEER EXCHANGE
20 Washington Square North
New York, NY 10011
Contact: Leslie Goebel
(212) 260-6250

This special "exchange" offers a service whereby volunteers escort seniors to doctor's appointments, to the bank, the store, or on other errands. This is a pleasant opportunity for those who would like to assist someone on a one-to-one basis outside of a structured center, perhaps even on an extended lunch hour. Responsible teens (over 16) can also volunteer. Interview.

CITIZENS CARE COMMITTEE
220 W. 143rd St.
New York, NY 10035
Contact: Ms. Holland, Director
(212) 410-0333

This committee provides nutrition and activities to local seniors. There are several Upper Manhattan locations that use volunteers in a number of areas, including clerical work, serving food, helping escort the seniors, and assisting with various activities such as exercise, arts and crafts, games, Bingo, dance groups, pool, and more. The schedule is flexible and you can work anytime between 9 A.M. and 4 P.M., when the centers are open. Interview, medical clearance; should have experience working with seniors. Some training will be given.

COUNCIL CENTER FOR SENIOR CITIZENS
1001 Quentin Rd.
Brooklyn, NY 11223
Contact: Judy Benas, Director of Volunteers
(718) 627-7680

One of the largest centers in New York, with over 5,000 residents, this center provides over 50 activities a week. Group activity leaders teach and assist in dance, arts and crafts, singing, and more. Any number of special skills are welcomed. Bilingual volunteers who can teach English as a second language are always needed. If you'd like to offer an activity, prepare a proposal and submit it with your résumé. The center's open to good suggestions. Interview, references.

COUNCIL SENIOR CENTER
241 W. 72nd St.
New York, NY 10023
Contact: Gary Perkins
(212) 799-7205

This senior center utilizes midweek volunteers to teach classes in areas such as pottery, sculpture, drawing, and other forms of artistic expression. If you are proficient at a skill, can articulate it well, and have patience, you might enjoy teaching seniors. Interview, orientation.

DAUGHTERS OF JACOB GERIATRIC CENTER
1160 Teller Ave.
Bronx, NY 10458
Contact: Sylvia Broader, Volunteer Coordinator
(718) 293-1500, ext. 218

This major geriatric center offers the elderly a number of services, from housing to social events. As a volunteer you can assist nurses in feeding and transporting patients and provide activities and recreation. Daughters of Jacob asks for a commitment of at least one four-hour shift per week. Application, two letters of reference, interview, orientation. Training is provided by the staff.

DeWITT NURSING HOME
211 E. 79th St.
New York, NY 10028
Contact: Jane Murphy, Director of Activities
(212) 879-1600, ext. 368

If you have a decent singing voice or another skill, or can just provide company, the DeWitt Nursing Home would love to have you volunteer. This 500-bed Upper East Side Manhattan facility provides care for the elderly. Volunteers are always sought to run recreational activities. Also, reading aloud, one-on-one friendly visits, escorts throughout the facility, and various types of entertainers are welcome. The director emphasizes a need for people who can entertain, noting that "strolling minstrels were a big hit." Interview, references.

DORCHESTER SENIOR CITIZENS HOME
1419 Dorchester Rd.
Bronx, NY 11226
Contact: Janet Schur, Director
(718) 941-6700
This long-standing establishment has special groups for blind seniors and utilizes volunteers who are comfortable working with the blind. Duties include talking to patients, helping with car services, making coffee, serving meals, and reading mail for the group. Interviews and on-premises training.

DOROT UNIVERSITY WITHOUT WALLS
171 W. 85th St.
New York, NY 10024
Contact: Timar Landis, Director of Volunteers
(212) 769-2850
Dorot (the Hebrew word meaning "generations") provides social, cultural, and educational opportunities to the elderly. After nearly 20 years, they have some 2,500 volunteers—who could include you.

The volunteer education program asks for teachers to teach classes over the phone to homebound people in the (212), (718), (516), or (914) area code. Topics range broadly. Obviously a good phone manner, speaking voice, and knowledge of the subject are preferred. This program operates weekdays from 9 A.M. to 5 P.M. Other programs include friendly visiting, holiday package deliveries, In-Sight (a program helping visually impaired elders), a homelessness prevention program, Project Open (case management and recreational programs to seniors in Lincoln Towers), street fairs, cemetery visits, and a caregiving center. Office work is also available, and there's even a calendar of special volunteer events for those who aren't able to commit to a regular schedule. Interview, training.

ENCORE COMMUNITY SERVICES
239 W. 49th St.
New York, NY 10019
Contact: Sister Teresa O'Connell
(212) 581-4224

Encore provides visitors and companionship to the elderly in the midtown Manhattan area. Volunteers take walks with, visit, and read to the elderly, as well as assisting them in other ways. Encore asks for a three-hour weekly minimum commitment. The midtown location allows for volunteer opportunities near the office for many nine-to-fivers. Interview and screening.

FLORENCE NIGHTINGALE NURSING HOME
1760 Third Ave.
New York, NY 10029
Contact: Linda Rodriguez, Activities Supervisor
(212) 410-8748

Featuring a holistic approach to long-term care, this 561-resident facility looks for volunteers as companions, to accompany residents on outings, to read to them, and to visit. Convenient for those who work in Manhattan and want to give a few hours before, after, or during the nine-to-five day. Interview, screening, medical requirements.

FRANCES SCHERVIER HOME AND HOSPITAL
2975 Independence Ave.
Bronx, NY 10463
Contact: Patricia G. Horgan, Director of Volunteer Services
(718) 548-1700

Come to their cabaret, my friend!

The facility provides a number of services to the elderly; it also offers an interesting array of volunteer opportunities. If you play piano you can entertain at cabaret nights; if not musically talented, you can help by serving wine and cheese to residents. If you like fun and games, you can assist in the Card Club; residents play cards and other games. Other volunteers help with feeding, transporting patients, providing companionship, or working in the office or the library. Application, interview, medical report required.

THE HEBREW HOME FOR THE AGED AT RIVERDALE
5901 Palisades Ave.
Riverdale, NY 10471
Contact: Gwynne J. Berkowitz, Volunteer Coordinator
(212) 549-8700

The Hebrew Home is set up to meet the needs of the elderly in the Riverdale area. Volunteers can devote a few hours to helping in the office with computer programming, administration, answering phones, and various clerical duties. Friendly visitors and transport assistants also help the staff with the residents. Interview, medical requirements.

ISABELLA GERIATRIC CENTER
515 Audubon Ave.
New York, NY 10040
Contact: Rema Sessler, Director of Volunteer Services
(212) 781-9800, ext. 485

Located in upper Manhattan, this is one of the largest geriatric centers in the city. They use an intergenerational group of volunteers from teens to members of the Retired Senior Volunteer Program (RSVP). Friendly visitors are always appreciated; office help is also needed; or you can work with patients in the area of recreation or assist the nursing staff. Application, interview, medical requirements, and personal references.

JACKSON HEIGHTS—ELMHURST KEHILLAH
35-68 87th St.
Jackson Heights, NY 11372
Contact: Naomi Cohen
(718) 457-4591

A Russian-American facility, the center provides educational workshops and services to seniors plus concerts and other activities. They ask volunteers to come in to speak Russian with immigrants and discuss topics of interest, including current events. Obviously, fluency in Russian is necessary. Interview and screening.

JASA-SEAGIRT HOUSE
1915 Seagirt Blvd.
Far Rockaway, NY 11691
Contact: Arlene Schalet
(718) 327-9453

The center provides social services for seniors including both recreational and counseling services. Volunteering at JASA-Seagirt means bringing enrichment to seniors through cultural activities, physical activities, or companionship. Also important is assisting in practical and daily projects such as letter writing, reading, and shopping. You need only be available two hours a week to teach writing to seniors. Interview, screening.

JEWISH HOME AND HOSPITAL FOR THE AGED
100 W. Kingsbridge Rd.
Bronx, NY 10468
Contact: Joyce Sauer, Director of Volunteer Services
(718) 579-0271

This multifaceted facility provides housing, day care, rehabilitation, and recreation for seniors. Several programs use volunteers, including the Phone a Friend program and feeding program. You can also help out in the nursing unit, in the office (doing clerical work), or as a friendly visitor. Interview; personal and medical references.

LONG ISLAND CARE CENTER
144-61 38th Ave.
Flushing, NY 11354
Contact: Denice Baratta, Director of Recreation and Volunteers
(718) 939-7500

A 200-bed facility that opened in 1969, the center offers residents many activities volunteers help to run, such as bingo and parties. Volunteers also help transport residents to therapy sessions, meals, and activities. Companionship and friendly visits are also provided. Since there is a large Asian population in Flushing, bilingual volunteers who speak Chinese or Korean are always appreciated. You will be trained in fire safety, taking care of the elderly, recognizing emergency situations, and other aspects of working in this type of facility. Minimum age 16. Interview, medical references, proof of TB test.

METHODIST CHURCH HOME FOR THE AGED
4499 Manhattan College Parkway
Bronx, NY 10471
Contact: Diane Morgan
(718) 580-5100, ext. 225

A 120-bed skilled-nursing facility, the Methodist Church Home offers you an opportunity to work with patients by feeding and transporting them; there is also a wealth of office work and more. Volunteers help out Monday–Saturday between 9 A.M. and 5 P.M., so you need to have a few daytime hours available. If you have a special skill that you can teach seniors, you might want to take your expertise into this facility. Art, music, gardening, and other skills are taught regularly. If you do not possess such a talent, you might opt to be a friendly visitor and read to, write letters for, or simply converse with residents. Interview, medical requirements.

NORTHEAST SENIOR SERVICE
45-50 195th St.
Flushing, NY 11358
Contact: Trudy McDaniels
(718) 357-4903

Formerly the Bayside Senior Assistance Center, this case management agency is approaching 20 years of serving the senior population in the community. It offers people over the age of 60 transportation to doctors and other appointments, and provides weekly correspondence and Meals on Wheels. Volunteers help by communicating via telephone, answering questions, and providing support and reassurance. Junior volunteers from neighborhood high schools help staff members (who drive seniors to stores) by assisting in shopping and carrying packages. Application, interview, references, medical clearance.

THE PARKER JEWISH GERIATRIC INSTITUTE
271-11 76th Ave.
New Hyde Park, NY 11040
Contact: Iris Schwartz, Volunteer Coordinator
(718) 343-2100

Friendly visitors are welcome to share their hobbies, entertain, teach, or provide companionship at this medical and nursing center, which provides short-term treatment and long-term home health care. There is also work for volunteers in the Alzheimer's Respite Center, as well as clerical assignments and sales opportunities in the gift shop. The facility asks for a minimum of three hours per week. Interview and training.

PENN SOUTH PROGRAM FOR SENIORS
290 Ninth Ave.
New York, NY 10001
Contact: Faye Glazer, Director of Volunteers
(212) 243-3670

As people advance in age, they often need assistance in their homes. And that's where you come in. The Penn South Program for Seniors provides on-site group activities, health care, and case management for 5,000 elderly residents of Mutual Redevelopment Houses, a moderate-income 10-building cooperative in Chelsea that has been called a "naturally occurring retirement community." Community-based volunteers, including elderly residents in good health, provide telephone reassurance, friendly visiting and help with transportation for frail or ailing residents. As a volunteer you can also teach classes, present art exhibits, help with the lending library, or distribute holiday packages. Interview, screening.

PROJECT EZRA
197 E. Broadway
New York, NY 10002
Contact: Rina Pianko, Volunteer Coordinator
(212) 982-4124

An independent community-based enterprise, Project Ezra serves the elderly on the Lower East Side. Volunteers are needed as friendly visitors to provide companionship to homebound and isolated Jewish seniors. Warm, friendly individuals with patience are preferred. Weekday hours, evenings, and Sundays are all available to volunteers. Once accepted to the program, you will be matched with a senior who has similar interests. Interview, references.

PROSPECT PARK NURSING HOME
1455 Coney Island Ave.
Brooklyn, NY 11230
Contact: Arnie Idelson, Director of Volunteers
(718) 352-9800

Actually located in the Midwood section of Brooklyn, in what was once the Vogue Theater, this nursing home welcomes volunteers to come in a few hours a week and help feed elderly patients. Also, volunteers make companion visits and read to patients. Bilingual skills are an asset. The center also has an intergenerational program: four high schools bring in students to visit as companions. Interview, medical requirements for feeding program.

SEARCH AND CARE
316 E. 88th St.
New York, NY 10128
Contact: Charlette Parkinson, Volunteer Coordinator
(212) 860-4145

Search and Care, a small agency, utilizes volunteers throughout the neighborhood for friendly home visits. It also organizes five or six outings a year to places such as the Conservatory in Central Park, Gracie Mansion, the Brooklyn Botanical Gardens and so on. These outings also need volunteer assistance. A few hours a week is all it takes. Search and Care tries to carefully match client and volunteer. Interview, training, medical requirement.

SILVERCREST EXTENDED CARE FACILITY
144-45 87th Ave.
Jamaica, NY 11435
Contact: Social Service Department
(718) 480-4000

A skilled-nursing facility, this is an opportunity for volunteers to assist residents with preparing for and conducting daily activities from writing letters to handling their finances. You can read their mail or favorite magazine to them. You can also help by escorting residents and visitors to and from the facility. Silvercrest asks for a minimum of four hours per week. Interview, references.

SUNNYSIDE HOME CARE
43-31 39th St.
Long Island City, NY 11104
Contact: Jane Schacker
(718) 784-6160, ext. 319

This agency provides home care and outreach services to those who can't get around because of illness or frailty. As a volunteer you will provide social activities or friendly visits to homebound clients. The center requests a four-hour weekly minimum commitment. Interview.

TOLENSTINE ZEISER COMMUNITY LIFE CENTER
2345 University Ave.
Bronx, NY 10468
Contact: Sister Margaret McDermott, Executive Director
(718) 933-3305

The center, which serves the University Heights section of the Bronx, provides a number of services ranging from day care to senior care. Volunteers are most often needed in the senior citizens center, serving lunches and helping with a variety of activities. This not-for-profit agency also runs a homeless center, soup kitchen, and Meals on Wheels program, all of which use volunteers to serve food. Interview, medical requirements for food service volunteers, training.

TOMPKINS SENIOR CENTER
550 Greene Ave.
Brooklyn, NY 11216
Contact: Queenie Thomas, Director
(718) 638-3000

A staple of the community, this 23-year-old senior center in Bedford Stuyvesant offers senior citizens excellent care. Volunteers can give a few hours a week in the food services division, or helping in the facility's office by doing clerical and administrative work. You can also help with arts-and-crafts activities or as an escort helping patients around the center. Interviews, medical requirements, references.

TREMONT COMMUNITY CENTER
Senior Citizens Center
2070 Clinton Ave.
Bronx, NY 10457
Contact: Thomas L. Guess, Executive Director
(718) 933-3716

This medium-sized 25-year-old facility uses volunteers in the dining room serving food. You can also give a few hours of your time per week, teaching and assisting with arts and crafts and similar activities. Clerical help is needed as well. Interviews; medical requirements required for food services.

UNITED NEIGHBORS OF EAST MIDTOWN
310 E. 42nd St.
New York, NY 10017
Contact: Cynthia Perry
(212) 682-1830

United Neighbors helps the elderly by providing food, companionship, escorts, and case evaluations. The Meals on Heels Program has volunteers preparing and delivering food to the elderly in the neighborhood. The program operates on Saturday mornings from the Presbyterian church on Fifth

Avenue. Deliveries are made in pairs. United Neighbors also has a friendly visitors program providing companionship, escorting elderly residents to the doctor, helping them get their shopping done, and so on. An intergenerational program offers high school students the opportunity to videotape the life stories of elderly clients. It's a great way for teens to get involved while learning from the experience. Parents with a teenage son or daughter can make this a family volunteer experience. Interview, references.

WEME/MAINSTREAM NUTRITION AND HEALTH CENTER
263 W. 86th St.
New York, NY 10024
Contact: Sherri Partridge
(212) 874-3750

The center operates a friendly visitor program; volunteers meet weekly with seniors. providing companionship and helping frail older adults who live alone with shopping and other necessities. Most important, you will be offering them an ear. The hours are negotiated between client and volunteer. Interview.

WILLIAM HODSON SENIOR CENTER
1320 Webster Ave.
Bronx, NY 10456
Contact: Tecla Brown, Volunteer Director
(718) 538-3700

A multipurpose center, Hodson provides activities, meals, recreation, and education for people over 60 years of age. If you have a creative skill such as knitting, crocheting, painting, or ceramics and can teach, you might opt to assist these seniors in such enjoyable and often therapeutic endeavors. It's important to relate well to seniors and have some leadership abilities. Interview, orientation.

12

Health and Human Services

From Hospitals and Clinics to Working with AIDS Patients

New York City has some of the largest, most technically advanced hospitals in the world, specializing in everything from pediatrics to plastic surgery. Many such institutions were originally founded by—and grew thanks to the efforts of—volunteers.

Hospitals are 24-hour facilities. This allows most to offer weekday, evening, and weekend volunteer opportunities. Although there are numerous positions available, it's not uncommon to find a waiting list to volunteer at a hospital on the weekends or in certain areas of interest. Don't be discouraged if there are no immediate openings. There is a significant amount of turnover, as many volunteers are young men and women getting their feet wet before venturing into medical school or other areas in the health field.

Hospital work ranges from patient contact, which includes assisting the nursing staff, to office, administrative, and clerical duties, to working in the library, research labs, and gift shops. It's important that you determine ahead of time what appeals to you. And remember, you need not remain in one area. Patient-care volunteers often experience some level of burnout after a year or two, but that doesn't mean another area of the hospital isn't awaiting their services.

Why the Health Field?

Gloria Deucher of the Jack D. Weiller Hospital of the Albert Einstein College of Medicine in the Bronx talks about her experience with volunteers. "People come in for a variety of reasons. In recent years we've been seeing a lot who work in financial institutions or similar professions who have become disenchanted, and they need to do something after work or on the weekend so they can have that human contact. We also get people who are thinking of possibly going into health care and they want to get a feel for a new job opportunity or career opportunity. Others are already in school and are looking to supplement what they're learning in the classroom with some kind of volunteer experience."

What Makes a Good Hospital Volunteer?

The ability not to become too attached is a positive trait for someone working in a hospital, and especially if he or she works with HIV/AIDS patients or in a hospice. However, there is an emotional side to all of us and sometimes remaining detached is difficult.

Gloria Deucher expounds on the personalities of hospital volunteers: "Working directly with patients, especially in pediatrics, the possibility of becoming emotionally attached always exists. You can't tell someone not to feel something, because you don't want automatons walking around. After all, volunteers are here to provide a certain amount of emotional support and connection. Hopefully the facility in which they work will provide support for their volunteers as far as that's concerned—workshops and group meetings and things like that."

Beyond Hospitals

Volunteers find positions working not only in hospitals but also in clinics, including some of the city's premier mental health facilities. There are also outreach programs that help homebound and HIV/AIDS patients.

Volunteers in the field of HIV/AIDS are very often those who have been affected by the loss of someone close to them. For some the work is a way of bringing into focus the realities of HIV/AIDS, while for others it's a step toward helping to fight this deadly disease and the alienation so many of those afflicted suffer.

Philip Santora of the Gay Men's Health Crisis says of the organization's massive volunteer program, "Some people want to give something back to the community, others want to help because someone that they know has been helped by GMHC, and some simply don't want to sit around anymore. We also get professionals who want more experience working around the area of HIV/AIDS. Professionals also help by giving massages, cutting hair, assisting with legal matters and entitlements, and more."

Tips on Volunteering in a Health Facility

▼ *Be uplifting and positive around patients.* Being sick or slowly recovering from an illness can be depressing and often discouraging. Any cheer you can provide may make more of a difference than you realize.

▼ *Defer to the staff in instances of any medical needs, including medications and dietary questions or requests.* In other words, if the patient asks for anything from a cup of tea to a piece of chocolate, make sure it's permitted on his or her diet as dictated by the doctor.

▼ *Know a patient's limitations, as well as your own.* Don't take on the responsibilities of the nursing staff.

▼ *Determine your own level of comfort and what you can and cannot do.* If you are squeamish you're better suited for the hospital reception desk or library than for working in the emergency room. Be realistic, and remember that giving your time in *any* capacity is important to the facility.

▼ *Be a good listener, yield to family members if they want to spend time with a patient, and most of all, be flexible.* Hospitals in New York City can be hectic places; schedules, rooms, and other aspects of your routine can and will change from time to time and from need to need.

Volunteering with HIV/AIDS Patients

People who want to work with HIV/AIDS patients are generally screened and given some orientation. If during this time, you find that you are afraid or uncomfortable, then this is not the volunteer opportunity for you. You can, however, work in areas associated with HIV/AIDS awareness and fund-raising. Philip Santora of GMHC explains that "a lot of people have a genuine desire to do buddy or hot-line work—[but] it really is a very heavy emotional gravity. To volunteer successfully [as a buddy] you have to have the time to develop a one-on-one relationship. . . . These people are going to count on you and it's something that can't be taken lightly."

Volunteering for Research Funding Organizations

Also addressing issues of health are an abundance of charitable organizations, many of which are national and have New York branches. Primarily, these organizations raise funds to fight a variety of illnesses.

Volunteers in this arena quite often make new friendships as they work together for a common cause. Although the amount of time you spend and your overall involvement will vary over the years, most who get involved with these organizations and foundations continue as active members for many years.

Working with the Disabled

Individuals with disabilities often need your assistance to circumvent the barriers set up by a society that is only recently recognizing their rights. Others want to partake in activities often limited or difficult for them.

As a volunteer you can read to the blind or tutor, mentor, escort, and otherwise assist the disabled through a large number of organizations around New York City.

Many volunteers in this area are looking to explore the growing area of physical therapy, while others are concerned about the role of the disabled population in our society. Whatever the reason, becoming involved helps people fulfill their potential, on both sides of the association.

Tips on Helping the Disabled

▼ *Identify a person by whom he or she is and not by his or her disability.*

▼ *Do not "overvolunteer."* In most cases people will ask for help when they need it.

▼ *Be respectful and encourage independence.* Remember that just be-

cause someone has a physical disability, it does not mean
he or she is not as mentally sharp as you are.

▼ *Don't make assumptions about what people's limits are, whether you
are dealing with physical or mental disabilities.*

Listings

HOSPITALS / OTHER HEALTH
FACILITIES / HIV / AIDS WORK

Hospitals and other health facilities listed below are required
by the state to have volunteers provide medical references
and be tested for TB and in some cases other diseases. Often,
after you've been accepted to work in the hospital, such testing is provided free of charge. Although it often seems like a
lot to go through to get involved, it's really not, considering
the benefits you'll receive from working in a hospital and the
bonds you'll form with other volunteers and even staff members.

ACTORS FUND OF AMERICA
1501 Broadway
Suite 518
New York, NY 10036
Contact: Joseph Ripple
(212) 221-7300
The Actors Fund offers a variety of services for people in the
arts. There are a host of ways to volunteer, from buddy programs for the elderly and HIV/AIDS patients to writing for
the fund's national newsletter. Clerical help is an ongoing
need, and those with specialized skills willing to work on a
pro bono basis as massage therapists, haircutters, or in other
capacities are welcome. If you're in the arts and interested in
helping your fellow artists, you can call for an interview.

THE AMERICAN RED CROSS OF GREATER NEW YORK
Volunteer Resources
150 Amsterdam Ave.
New York, NY 10023
Contact: Volunteer Department
(212) 787-1000

Every minute, every hour they are helping someone in need, and their nearly 2,600 volunteers are not enough. The American Red Cross of Greater New York provides critical services to the metropolitan area. According to Red Cross statistics, an average of ten disasters, primarily residential fires, happen in New York City every day. Opportunities are available in all five boroughs for disaster relief volunteers to reassure and assist victims, conduct damage assessments of dwellings, transport families to temporary housing, serve meals to victims and relief workers, arrange for clothing and food for families, and perform other duties. It's preferable that you be able to handle stressful situations well. There are also senior services, homeless services, and military and social services. Interview, screening; training where necessary.

See also chapter 5, "Education."

BAYLEY SETON HOSPITAL
75 Vanderbilt Ave.
Staten Island, NY 10304
Contact: Joan DeMarco
(718) 390-5522

This small (192-bed) hospital provides a cordial atmosphere for volunteering in the health field. Bayley Seton offers three main areas for volunteers: clerical work; patient care, which includes transporting, feeding, and visiting patients and even baby-sitting for clinic patients; and finally gift shop sales assistance. Volunteers are asked to put in at least four hours a week. Junior volunteers (14–18 years old) are also welcome, and must provide working papers. Interview, medical references; some medical testing is provided by the hospital.

BENSONHURST VOLUNTEER AMBULANCE SERVICES
8161 New Utrecht Ave.
Brooklyn, NY 11214
Contact: Tara Alegrio, Director of Personnel
(718) 837-3912

Ideal for young people (14 to 25) looking to venture into medicine-related careers, the ambulance service has volunteer programs that train dispatchers and personnel to ride their ambulances. EMT or First Response certification is required and shifts are four hours. The youth squad offers 14- to 18-year-olds the opportunity to train while helping with fund-raising drives and taking blood pressure. The senior squad is for those 18 and up. Volunteering here is a great way to determine if the health field is for you. Training.

BETH ABRAHAM HOSPITAL
612 Allerton Ave.
Bronx, NY 10467
Contact: Anne Richter, Director of Volunteer Services
(718) 920-5933

There are a wealth of opportunities for volunteers at this hospital, including working in the dental clinic, pharmacy, activities center, mail room, print shop, or library; helping with feeding, occupational therapy, or physical therapy; escorting or transporting patients; or assisting the staff in any number of other areas. Student volunteers are welcome but must have a parental release form and working papers. Two personal references, medical reference, medical requirements.

BETH ISRAEL MEDICAL CENTER
First Avenue and 16th St.
New York, NY 10003
Contact: Terri Rizzo, Director of Volunteer Services
(212) 420-2733

Beth Israel uses volunteers for working with patients as well as in non-patient-related areas. It also has outreach programs to the elderly; volunteers help by telephoning and visiting discharged patients, who are recovering in their homes. The range is broad and the hospital prefers that volunteers come in for an interview to discuss the many possible programs. Volunteers are asked for a minimum six-month commitment. Interview, medical requirements, personal references.

You can also contact the Beth Israel Medical Center North Division at (212) 628-4769. Ask for the assistant director of volunteer services, Mariadora Caputo.

BROADWAY CARES/EQUITY FIGHTS AIDS
165 W. 46th St.
New York, NY 10036
Contact: Volunteer Coordinator
(212) 840-0770

Broadway Cares/EFA is the theatrical industry's largest fund-raising organization for people with AIDS, providing direct personal grants to people throughout the entertainment industry, from ticket takers to producers. An event-driven organization, Broadway Cares utilizes its nearly 250 volunteers to help with special mailings and to assist at events, including the large annual Broadway Flea Market and Grand Auction at Shubert Alley. Volunteers are called when they are needed, rather than making an ongoing weekly time commitment. It's a wonderful way for people with an interest in the theater to get involved in helping fight the AIDS crisis. Interview.

BRONX-LEBANON HOSPITAL
1257 Fulton Ave.
Bronx, NY 10456
Contact: Betty Cole, Director of Volunteer Services
(718) 590-1800

One of the borough's busiest hospitals, Bronx-Lebanon uses nursing floor assistants to help make beds, transport and feed patients, and run various errands. Friendly visitors to HIV/AIDS patients, clerical help, and library assistants are also welcome. The hospital requests a minimum commitment of three hours per week. Interview, medical requirements; hospital will provide some medical tests.

BRONX MUNICIPAL HOSPITAL CENTER
Room 156
Jacobi Hospital
Pelham Pkwy. South and Eastchester Rd.
Bronx, NY 10461
Contact: Vivian Storey, Assistant Director of Auxiliary and Volunteer
  Services
(718) 918-5000
Sitting on a 64-acre campus, the 800-bed facility offers numerous volunteer opportunities. You can work as a patient escort, help in food services, housekeeping or fund-raising, or work in the gift shop. There is also a need for bilingual volunteers who speak fluent French, Spanish, Hebrew, or Yiddish. Students may volunteer starting at the age of 16. The hospital asks for a four-hour minimum commitment per week and offers an ongoing in-house training program. It also requires a physical exam, which is provided by the employee health service.

THE BROOKDALE HOSPITAL CENTER
525 Rockaway Pkwy.
Second Floor
Brooklyn, NY 11212
Contact: Anne Dubno, Director of Volunteer Services
(718) 240-5277
One of Brooklyn's premier medical facilities, Brookdale has various volunteer opportunities available. Baby cuddlers hold and cuddle boarder babies, or you can donate your time as a patient aide or clerical assistant. Several other programs available. Interview, screening, medical requirements.

CABRINI MEDICAL CENTER
227 E. 19th St.
New York, NY 10003
Contact: Joyce Rod, Volunteer Coordinator
(212) 995-6000
This 499-bed acute-care hospital is over 100 years old and is the self-proclaimed "cleanest hospital in New York." Volunteer opportunities basically comprise helping the staff in all

areas. There are patient-related services such as issuing library cards, providing companionship, and more. Non-patient-related activities include assisting in administrative areas. Interview, medical requirements, references.

CENTER FOR SAFETY IN THE ARTS
5 Beekman St.
Suite 820
New York, NY 10038
Contact: Angela Babin
(212) 227-6220

This unique organization provides health and safety information to artists as well as schools and museums. Health hazards are uncovered and safety is promoted. The center welcomes volunteers to assist with clerical work, data entry, and various other office tasks. Computer skills are helpful, and an affinity for the arts is certainly welcome, although not a requirement. Interview.

THE CENTRAL PARK MEDICAL UNIT
Volunteer Ambulance Unit
P.O. Box 440, Gracie Station
New York, NY 10028
Contact: Rafael Castellanos, President
(212) 860-8024

If you want to take your interest in medicine outdoors, why not venture into the world's busiest park and help the Central Park Medical Unit? This all-volunteer ambulance unit provides swift professional medical assistance to those in need. CPMU volunteers respond to nearly 1,000 medical emergencies a year. If you are a certified emergency medical technician and have experience in life-threatening situations, you can become a part of this exciting team. Members are not strictly from the medical community. They include people from all walks of life: lawyers, musicians, librarians, actors—all certified EMTs. CPMU members participate in monthly in-service training to stay abreast of the latest medical procedures and hone their skills. Interview.

DISCIPLESHIP OUTREACH CENTER
5711 Fourth Ave.
Brooklyn, NY 11220
Contact: Volunteer Coordinator
(718) 492-4436

The center provides HIV/AIDS support, substance abuse programs, drug counseling, and case management. Volunteers are asked to visit clients in their homes and/or take them for walks or for planned activities once a week. Good listening skills are very important, but the center urges that volunteers *not* give counseling. Applicants are asked to give a minimum of three hours per week. Interview, screening, training.

GAY MEN'S HEALTH CRISIS
129 W. 20th St.
New York, NY 10011
Contact: Philip Santora
Volunteer Intake (212) 337-3583
Volunteer Office (212) 337-3505

GMHC offers services to anyone affected by HIV. It has approximately 4,000 program volunteers. There are two categories of volunteer opportunities: client-related programs, and education, outreach, and administrative support programs. An additional 4,000 volunteers help promote the many GMHC political and special fund-raising activities including the annual Dance-a-thon and Aidswalk. Volunteering in the area of HIV/AIDS can be difficult for some; fully aware of that, GMHC offers people all levels of involvement. It is among the leading full-service AIDS organizations. Orientation, training, references including medical where necessary.

GOD'S LOVE WE DELIVER
166 Ave. of the Americas
New York, NY 10013
Contact: Linda Melnikoff, Volunteer Intake Specialist
(212) 865-4900

If helping to feed the many homebound people with AIDS interests you, then you might want to take part in this large program, which has over 50 food distribution centers throughout New York City and Hudson County, New Jersey. Preparing and delivering food are key elements to the program; to participate, a car is required in the boroughs outside Manhattan. You can also help with special events, clerical work, or mailings, or by providing holiday presents to clients. Volunteers will be placed in the center nearest their home or office. Interview.

GOLDWATER MEMORIAL HOSPITAL
Roosevelt Island
New York, NY 10044
Contact: Pamela Hargrow, Volunteer Coordinator
(212) 318-4457

If you're a Roosevelt Islander, love riding the tram or would simply like to volunteer at a major health facility, there are plenty of opportunities at 67-year-old Goldwater. This huge 984-bed hospital uses volunteers in all areas, including nursing and patient care, clerical and administrative work, physical and occupational therapy, and even in the gift shop. Training is necessary in most areas. Interview, medical requirements, references.

HEARTS AND VOICES
150 W. 80th St.
New York, NY 10024
Contact: Bonnie Sher, Program Director
(212) 799-4276

For the past five years this unique program has been bringing entertainment to the HIV/AIDS patients in several New York hospitals—to the tune(s) of over 1,800 performances. Shows generally run 30 minutes and include two singers and a piano player, but other talents are also featured, including jugglers, magicians, dancers, ventriloquists, and stand-up comics. If you have a talent, it's a marvelous way to brighten a patient's day while feeling good about yourself and enhancing your skills. And if you are not a performer, Hearts and Voices also welcomes volunteers who wish to regularly visit patients on a weekly or monthly basis, talking with them or escorting them to and from the performances. Interview; training where necessary.

HOSPITAL FOR JOINT DISEASES
301 E. 17th St.
New York, NY 10003
Contact: Director of Volunteer Services
(212) 598-6042

This is the nation's leading hospital specializing in musculo-skeletal, rheumatic, and neurological diseases in adults and children. Volunteer opportunities are plentiful. You can be a friendly visitor, an interpreter for foreign-born patients, a helper in the library or gift shop, a recreational therapy assistant, a tour guide, a nursing assistant, a housekeeping assistant, or an office or clerical worker—to name just a few possibilities. Everyone from college students to senior citizens is welcome to volunteer. Interview, two references, medical requirements.

HOSPITAL FOR SPECIAL SURGERY
535 E. 70th St.
New York, NY 10021
Contact: Wendy Yondorf, Supervisor of Volunteer Services
(212) 606-1000

An orthopedic facility, focusing primarily on arthritis and rheumatology, the hospital has a very active clinic. Various opportunities for volunteers include pediatric recreation, working in the patient library, assisting in occupational therapy, visiting patients, working in the gift shop, delivering flowers and gifts to patients, and assisting on the nursing floor. High school students are often used as nursing assistants. Interview, medical requirements.

HOUSING WORKS
594 Broadway
Suite 700
New York, NY 10012
Contact: Brigid Lang, Volunteer Coordinator
(212) 966-0466

Housing Works provides homes for over 500 people with HIV/AIDS, and offers a variety of programs. Volunteers provide hospital visits and companionship to patients as well as offering emotional support. Besides the Buddy Program, there are opportunities available in the thrift shop, in job training programs, and in advocacy, fund-raising and helping to plan and further develop Housing Works programs. Essentially, if you want to help people with HIV/AIDS, there is something you can do at Housing Works. The group asks that you give them a minimum commitment of a few hours a week for three months. Interview, references, orientation.

THE JACK D. WEILER HOSPITAL OF THE ALBERT EINSTEIN COLLEGE OF MEDICINE
1825 Eastchester Rd.
Bronx, NY 10461
Contact: Gloria Deucher, Director of Volunteer Services
(718) 904-2934

One of the largest hospitals in the Bronx, and certainly the one sporting the longest name, this facility offers a wealth of volunteer opportunities to work with a cordial, appreciative staff.

Office volunteers do clerical work and answer phones. There are opportunities to work on the nursing units—at nursing stations, or helping with recreational programs, assisting with feedings, or helping with patient transport. A host of other opportunities also exists in this busy major medical center. Interview, medical requirements, training where necessary. TB and other testing will be done at the hospital.

JAMAICA COMMUNITY SUPPORT SYSTEMS
165-15 88th Ave.
Jamaica, NY 11432
Contact: Compeer Coordinator
(718) 291-4848

This facility serves over 500 clients regularly. They provide a unique "compeer service" offering friendship and support to adults with emotional problems. Volunteers befriend a psychiatric patient who attends the Day Treatment Center or resides in an adult home. Patience, understanding, a knack for listening, and a positive outlook are the tools needed for those interested. Interview, personal references; training provided. For the first two months, volunteers work under supervision.

KINGSBROOK JEWISH MEDICAL CENTER
585 Schenectady Ave.
Brooklyn, NY 11203
Contact: Eve Spilman, Director of Volunteer Services
(718) 604-5766

Located in the Crown Heights section of Brooklyn, this multipurpose 70-year-old facility includes a 500-bed nursing home, adult day care center, rehabilitation centers (including physical therapy, speech therapy, and recreational therapy), and a 300-bed acute-care center. Volunteers help with patient care, support the nursing staff, implement and assist in recreational activities for patients, and help with library services and clerical tasks. Interview, medical requirements, orientation.

LENOX HILL HOSPITAL
100 E. 77th St.
New York, NY 10021
Contact: Hillary Ganton, Director of Volunteer Services
(212) 434-2600, ext. 238

Over 150 volunteer opportunities await you—on the nursing units, in the clinics, in the laboratory, at the information desk, in the library, or on the refreshment cart, which provides refreshments to the relatives of critically ill patients. There is even a plant cart, which brings plants to patients who may not have received flowers or visitors. All volunteers are asked to put in at least three consecutive daytime hours or two consecutive nighttime hours per week. There is also a very active program for premedical and pre–physical therapy students who want to familiarize themselves with the workings of a hospital. Interview, medical requirements, orientation; training for certain areas.

Health

LONG ISLAND COLLEGE HOSPITAL
358 Henry St.
Brooklyn, NY 11201
Contact: Barbara Ann Franco, Director of Volunteer Services
(718) 780-1982
LICH's meal companionship program offers encouragement and assistance to patients, while hospitality cart volunteers meet and bring cheer to patients throughout the facility. Other possibilities include patient education, waiting room and emergency room liaison work, the patient visitation service, recreational and diversional activities, pediatric storytelling, book reading, and a rape crisis intervention program. LICH wants to make the stressful experience of hospitalization less frightening for patients . . . and it does so with the help of volunteers. Interview, medical requirements, training according to position.

LUTHERAN MEDICAL CENTER
150 55th St.
Brooklyn, NY 11220
Contact: Bonnie Klima-Olsen, Administrator for Volunteer Initiatives
(718) 630-7296
In the Sunset Park section of Brooklyn near Bay Ridge, this 533-bed nonprofit hospital offers a host of volunteer programs.

You can help as a member of the Buddy Program, giving a six-month commitment to visiting HIV-positive patients. There are also opportunities to work as a liaison between the emergency room and the waiting area. You might also assist the nursing staff or work in the offices, providing clerical help. Interview, medical requirements, orientation; special training in certain areas.

MANHATTAN EYE, EAR, AND THROAT HOSPITAL
210 E. 64th St.
New York, NY 10021
Contact: Public Affairs Office
(212) 605-3713
Founded to meet the needs of people in the vicinity affected

by ear, nose, throat, and skin disorders, this 150-bed hospital has a 24-hour emergency room and performs the most plastic surgery in the world (be careful not to leave with a different face than you had when you started volunteering!) Opportunities range from working with patients to clerical work to assisting the staff. A member of the public affairs office will help you find an opportunity that is right for you. Hours are generally 9 A.M. to 5 P.M. Monday through Friday. Interview, medical requirements.

THE METHODIST HOSPITAL CENTER
506 Sixth Ave.
Brooklyn, NY 11215
Contact: Mimi Makovitzky, Director of Educational & Volunteer
  Resources
(718) 780-3397
This high-quality health care facility offers several volunteer opportunities. Telephone reassurance volunteers provide support and comfort to recently discharged patients. Friendly visitors provide companionship to HIV/AIDS patients. Emergency room facilitators help E.R. patients while reassuring and comforting their friends and family. The special Bedtime Story Project has volunteers reading and singing to pediatric patients. These are just a few of the many programs offered. Interview, medical requirements, training.

THE MOMENTUM PROJECT
155 W. 23rd St.
Eleventh Floor
New York, NY 10011
Contact: Judy Jenson
(212) 691-8100
Working in conjunction with several churches and a synagogue, the Momentum Project is designed to bring people who are HIV-positive together for communal meals. Volunteers help set tables, pack pantry bags, prepare food, do registration, work in the office, and help with fund-raising. There are eight locations throughout the city. There is an orientation program and on-site training.

MONTEFIORE MEDICAL CENTER
111 E. 210th St.
Bronx, NY 10467
Contact: Millie Izquierdo, Director of Volunteers
(718) 920-4191

This 100 + -year-old, 750-bed facility uses over 500 volunteers. Areas of patient contact include working in recreational and therapy programs that help children cope with illness; assisting with seniors' long-term care (from friendly visits to entertaining); helping the nursing staff; or working with HIV/AIDS patients in Montefiore's BRAVO program. From special events to office help, volunteer opportunities are abundant and meet a variety of schedules. The hospital asks for a minimum commitment of four hours weekly and at least 100 hours a year. Interview, personal references, medical requirements.

THE MOUNT SINAI MEDICAL CENTER
1 Gustave Levy Place (100th St. and Fifth Ave.)
New York, NY 10029
Contact: Cynthia Levy, Director of Volunteer Services
(212) 241-6288

The new state-of-the-art Guggenheim Pavilion is the latest addition to this 1,167-bed facility, which has been a fixture of Manhattan's Upper East Side since 1852. Numerous volunteer opportunities include assisting the staff with patient care and helping with administrative and office duties. The program is large and essentially offers a position to anyone interested in hospital volunteering. Interview, medical requirements, orientation, training if necessary.

NEW YORK BLOOD CENTER
150 Amsterdam Ave.
New York, NY 10023
Contact: Louise Greiner, Volunteer Coordinator
(212) 468-2030

The New York Blood Center welcomes friendly, outgoing volunteers to work on blood drives throughout the city. Blood Center volunteers greet and register blood donors, label forms, escort donors, observe donor reactions, and serve refreshments. The only requirement is that you be over 16 and comfortable working with people. And you will work at a number of interesting locations. Interview, training.

NEW YORK DOWNTOWN HOSPITAL
170 Williams St.
New York, NY 10038
Contact: Charissa Murray, Director of Volunteer Services
(212) 312-5000
Located just south of Chinatown, this 300-bed nonprofit hospital looks for volunteers to help with free health screenings in the community, to work at the security desk, and to help in the outpatient clinic. Also welcome are bilingual volunteers, especially those versed in Chinese. Downtown Hospital asks for a minimum 100-hour commitment, although the time frame is open. Interview, medical requirements, references.

THE NEW YORK EYE AND EAR INFIRMARY
Second Ave. at 14th St.
New York, NY 10003
Contact: Volunteer Services Department
(212) 979-4462
Focusing on the treatment of eye, ear, nose, and throat problems, the infirmary uses over 200 volunteers, who work in administration, accounting, ambulatory care, food services, housekeeping, glaucoma services, medical records, nursing and patient services, information services, personnel, communication, and more. Once you apply, someone will meet with you to learn your interests and skills. Interview, personal references, medical requirements. TB and rubella tests can be done at the infirmary.

THE NEW YORK HOSPITAL
525 E. 68th St.
New York, NY 10021
Contact: Camille Tumolo, Director of Volunteer Services
(212) 746-4396
The New York Hospital is one of the largest and most comprehensive in the country. Volunteers participate in patient

care, giving mealtime assistance, helping with recreational therapy, reassuring patients, working on the hospital gift cart, and so on. There are other opportunities in the administrative end, at the gift shop, and in teaching classes. Interview, medical requirements, references.

NEW YORK UNIVERSITY MEDICAL CENTER
550 First Ave.
New York, NY 10016
Contact: Richard Elefonte, Volunteer Coordinator
(212) 263-6100

Another of New York's significant, bustling hospitals, NYU Medical Center offers a vast number of opportunities for volunteers. There are about 40 to 50 placement areas throughout the hospital, including patient areas, nursing units, visiting programs, information desks, the gift shop, the library, the offices, and administrative areas. The facility asks for at least a four-hour shift per week and a 100-hour overall time commitment. Interview, medical requirements, training where necessary.

THE POSTGRADUATE CENTER FOR MENTAL HEALTH
124 E. 28th St.
New York, NY 10016
Contact: Irwin Schwartz, Volunteer Coordinator
(212) 576-4100

Founded in 1945, this is one of the largest nonprofit mental health and rehabilitation centers in the country. It provides individual and group psychotherapy and vocational rehabilitation, and house an ethnically diverse population of all ages. Working in a comfortable, supportive environment, you can use your skills in any of a number of areas including word processing, public relations, advertising, marketing, tutoring, photography, film and video productions, retailing, law, or library work. Perhaps the most rewarding of the volunteer services is the mentor program, which will have you working directly with clients under the direction of therapists and vocational counselors. Interview, training.

RIVERBAY COMMUNITY VOLUNTEER AMBULANCE CORPS.
100-26 Debs Place
Bronx, NY 10475
Contact: Alan Berger, President
(718) 671-6583

For those ready to learn and take on health-related responsibilities, this outfit uses volunteers to drive and/or work as "techs" on the ambulances. Volunteers are trained in CPR and other areas of medical and safety preparation. There is a youth squad for 16- to 18-year-olds. Hours are primarily weeknights although both day and evening shifts are offered on weekends. You must be ready to meet the challenges of these positions. Interview, training.

RONALD McDONALD HOUSE
404 E. 73rd St.
New York, NY 10021
Contact: Denise Bomberger, Administrative Director, Volunteer
   Services
(212) 472-0376

Volunteer involvement is what makes Ronald McDonald House a successful home away from home for children fighting cancer. Volunteers can work as part of the office staff, handling phone calls, clerical duties, typing and computer work, covering the reception desk and assisting with mailings. Office volunteers work a minimum of three hours per week during the business day.

"People-oriented" volunteers can help with the large sidewalk book sale campaign that generates funds for Ronald McDonald House. Those who would like to help in the evenings or on weekends can assist in recreational activities, including parties, arts and crafts, bingo, barbecues, and so on. For these assignments, it's important to have some experience working with children. The two primary requirements, however, are dependability and commitment. Interview, orientation.

ST. LUKE'S/ROOSEVELT HOSPITAL CENTER
St. Luke's:
Amsterdam Ave. at 114th St.
New York, NY 10025
Contact: Volunteer Department
(212) 523-2187
Roosevelt:
428 W. 59th St.
New York, NY 10019
Contact: Volunteer Department
(212) 523-7155

This two-location, 1,315-bed, private nonprofit hospital on Manhattan's Upper West Side welcomes volunteers 14 and over who provide medical references. Volunteer assignments are made by matching the interests of the volunteers and the needs of the hospital as closely as possible. You can assist with patient advocacy, work in the gift shop or the patient library, perform various types of office work, help with special projects, work as an HIV/AIDS volunteer, care for boarder babies, translate for non-English-speaking patients, read to patients, feed them, or provide companionship. Interview, medical requirements, training where necessary.

ST. VINCENT'S MEDICAL CENTER OF RICHMOND
355 Bard Ave.
Staten Island, NY 10310
Contact: Emily Vallelong, Director of Volunteer Services
(718) 876-2110

A major acute-care facility, St. Vincent's welcomes volunteers 14 years old and up. A special junior program offers high school students a chance to gain practical experience in the health field. Adult volunteers can assist in "Messenger Transport Services," handling pickups from the laboratories and pharmacy and acting as liaisons between departments. Volunteers also escort patients to religious services and assist in hospital administration. Interview, personal references, medical requirements.

STATEN ISLAND MENTAL HEALTH SOCIETY
CHAIT Clinic
669 Castleton Ave.
Staten Island, NY 10301
Contact: Fran Hogan, Director of Community Relations
(718) 442-2225

Staten Island's largest mental health facility, the CHAIT clinic focuses on children and teens. Programs range from day care for young children to mental health services for college students. As a volunteer, you can assist by tutoring youngsters in reading twice a week, working in the facility's thrift shops or in conjunction with the Women's Guild, and planning fund-raising activities (which include fashion shows and an annual ball). Interview, references; some training provided.

UNION HOSPITAL
260 E. 188th St.
Bronx, NY 10458
Contact: Anna L. York, Director of Volunteer Services
(718) 960-9000

If you love babies you might become a boarder baby volunteer, and assist in feeding, holding, hugging and cuddling babies. This busy facility also has an ongoing need for volunteers in the nursing unit or in many patient-related duties. If you'd prefer to remain behind the scenes, you can help with hospital administration, doing office and clerical work. Interview, medical requirements, personal references.

UNITED HOSPITAL FUND
350 Fifth Ave.
23rd Floor
New York, NY 10118
Contact: Volunteer Hotline
(212) 675-6644

The United Hospital Fund is a one-stop location for volunteering in the hospital nearest you. For over 60 years they have been placing good Samaritans in hospitals throughout the New York area.

In its role as a placement service the UHF will match your skills with the needs of a New York City hospital. It provides translators and has cuddler programs whereby volunteers hold babies in hospitals when the parents are not available. There are opportunities to work directly with patients: calming them before and after an operation; acting as a liaison between patients and hospital administrators; explaining entitlements or filling out Medicare or similar forms. These are just a few of the numerous opportunities that the UHF provides for those of you looking to give "a few hours a week" in the health field. Interview.

See also chapter 14, "Umbrella Organizations and Referral Services."

UPPER MANHATTAN MENTAL HEALTH CLINIC
1727 Amsterdam Ave.
New York, NY 10031
Contact: Volunteer Department
(212) 694-9200
This Upper West Side Manhattan facility asks for compeers to take clients out to the movies and otherwise to socialize with them as often as possible. The hours are very flexible, although it is preferred that you make a one-year commitment, for the sake of stability. Interview, references.

RESEARCH FUNDING ORGANIZATIONS

The listings below are primarily the New York affiliates or branches of larger national organizations, associations, or foundations. Besides those listed, there are numerous others looking to raise funds and help people. Some will want you to be a member, while others are simply glad you're there to help. Either way, they appreciate volunteers, and it's a gratifying way to get involved.

ALZHEIMER'S DISEASE AND RELATED DISORDERS ASSOCIATION
420 Lexington Ave.
Suite 610
New York, NY 10170
Contact: Gail Hoffman, Volunteer Coordinator
(212) 963-0700

Heading four local area chapters in Queens, Brooklyn, and the Bronx, this Manhattan-based association is one of 200 branches nationwide. The association provides education, counseling, and family support groups. Volunteers are needed to give companionship to patients and to give caretakers two-to four-hour respites. Volunteers are also trained to work the 24-hour telephone help line, which provides information about the disease and caregiving issues and assistance. Clerical help in the chapter offices and work on special projects such as fund-raising drives are also welcome. Interviews; extensive training provided in some areas.

AMERICAN CANCER SOCIETY
New York City Division
19 W. 56th St.
New York, NY 10019
Contact: Anne Hecht, Personnel Services and Training Coordinator
(212) 586-8700

The American Cancer Society is a nationwide volunteer organization dedicated to eliminating cancer as a major health problem.

A large organization, active throughout the city, the ACS has many volunteer opportunities, particularly in the areas of education and public awareness, fund-raising, special events, administrative work, phone and mailing duties, and much more. Special events such as the Paws Walk use a number of volunteers, not to mention dogs. A great deal of literature is available if you're interested. Interview.

The ACS's New York City division has unit offices in Brooklyn, the Bronx, and Staten Island as well as Manhattan. Queens has a separately run office; call (718) 263-2224.

See also chapter 5, "Education."

AMERICAN DIABETES ASSOCIATION—NEW YORK DOWNSTATE
149 Madison Ave.
New York, NY 10016
Contact: Marie Kaplowitz
(212) 725-4925, ext. 245

The New York chapter of this nationwide association utilizes volunteers to help with phone work, mailings, computer data entry, and special events. Fund-raising endeavors always welcome volunteer contributors. Volunteers are asked to sign up to work one day a week, or at least, a few hours on a regular basis. Interview.

AMERICAN HEART ASSOCIATION: NEW YORK CITY AFFILIATE
122 E. 42nd St.
New York, NY 10168
Contact: Catherine Meyers, Volunteer Administrator
(212) 661-5335

The New York City affiliate of the American Heart Association has been in existence for nearly 80 years and has always used a wealth of volunteers.

A relatively new volunteer program offers over 40 different options. Laypeople as well as health care professionals work in a variety of capacities, including the programming department, which helps deliver educational programs to schools as well as health care sites and community locations. Also, office assistants are always welcome. Additional volunteers are used for a number of major special events. There are weekend and evening programs for nine-to-fivers, and on-site and off-site opportunities throughout the five boroughs.

CANCER CARE
1180 Avenue of the Americas
New York, NY 10036
Contact: Loretta Dunn, Volunteer Coordinator
(212) 302-2400

Serving the tristate area, Cancer Care is a private, nonprofit social service agency with some 40 social workers helping patients and their families with individual and group therapy. Volunteers can work as friendly visitors, providing companionship to homebound cancer patients for two or three hours a week. Office volunteers help with mailings and administrative services. There is also a junior committee, which helps plan special events. Interviews.

GREATER NEW YORK CHAPTER OF THE MARCH OF DIMES
233 Park Ave. South
New York, NY 10003
Contact: Laura Henry, Manager of Volunteer Services
(212) 353-8353

Originally founded by President Franklin D. Roosevelt in 1938 to fight polio, the March of Dimes continues today in its efforts to help prevent birth defects. Among the many fund-raising activities is the annual Walk America, held the last Sunday in April. Volunteers are needed to work at check-in, help with refreshments, and marshal the walk route. There are also outreach programs and administrative opportunities with your volunteer name on them. Interview.

MUSCULAR DYSTROPHY ASSOCIATION, MANHATTAN DISTRICT
10 E. 40th St.
Suite 4110
New York, NY 10016
Contact: Jennifer Ricca, Program Coordinator
(212) 689-9040

You've seen Jerry Lewis and the telethon; now you, too, can help raise funds to fight muscular dystrophy as part of this high-profile organization funded almost entirely through the efforts of volunteers. The telethon is just one of numerous unusual and exciting events MDA plans throughout the year. Volunteers brainstorm on the planning committee to help originate such events, and volunteers are further needed to promote them, sell raffle tickets, work registration, set up and clean up, and answer phones. Administrative volunteers also get involved mailing out the MDA newsletter and with special-events mailings. Professionals play a major role in MDA as well. Interview.

The MDA's Lake Success branch handles the other four boroughs; you can, however, volunteer to work through ei-

ther office. The phone number of the Lake Success office is
(516) 358-1012.

NATIONAL NEUROFIBROMATOSIS FOUNDATION
95 Pine St.
New York, NY 10005
Contact: Kim Robinson
(212) 344-6633

This national organization, based in New York, has been
around nearly 20 years. A nonprofit foundation, it focuses on
helping to find a cure for neurofibromatosis. Volunteers help
with clerical duties, work on a variety of projects including
fund-raising events, and do mass mailings. Interested volunteers will receive orientation about the foundation. Interview.

THE NATIONAL HEMOPHILIA FOUNDATION
110 Greene St.
New York, NY 10012
Contact: Susan Levitt
(212) 219-8180

One of some 45 chapters nationwide, the New York branch
welcomes volunteers with computer knowledge to help in the
office. If you have library skills you can help in the library or
with research. Volunteers who help with mailings or special
events are also valuable contributors. Schedules are flexible.
Interview, references.

NATIONAL KIDNEY FOUNDATION OF NEW YORK/NEW JERSEY
1250 Broadway
New York, NY 10001
Contact: Loretta Haberman
(212) 629-9770

The only health agency dedicated to the eradication of kidney, urologic, and hypertensive diseases, the Kidney Foundation has been serving the New York/New Jersey area for over
40 years. Volunteers help with special events such as selling
raffle tickets for the annual new-car giveaway. Office help is
always welcome with mass mailings and other clerical duties.
The pediatric program has volunteers taking children to the

circus, pumpkin picking, or on other fun-filled excursions. Interview.

SLE (LUPUS) FOUNDATION
149 Madison Ave.
New York, NY 10016
Contact: Volunteer Office
(212) 685-4118

This nonprofit, membership foundation is dedicated to finding the cause of lupus, improving treatment, and finding a cure. It funds medical research and also works hard to assist patients' families and friends with the anxieties and frustrations that may be encountered when dealing with a chronic illness. As a volunteer you can help with phone and office work, fund-raising activities, and education about lupus. Interview, membership.

ORGANIZATIONS THAT HELP THE DISABLED

HOSPITAL AUDIENCES
220 W. 42nd St.
New York, NY 10036
Contact: Gina Rubino, Volunteer Coordinator
(212) 575-7667

Hospital Audiences is designed to provide access to cultural events for people with disabilities. Volunteers meet groups at theaters, arenas, and other venues. They help distribute tickets, assist in getting groups in and out of arenas, and handle any related problems. Volunteers need to be able to handle various situations that may arise at the events. Interview, orientation.

INTERNATIONAL CENTER FOR THE DISABLED
340 E. 24th St.
New York, NY 10010
Contact: Joanna Asperger, Volunteer Coordinator
(212) 679-0100

The International Center for the Disabled was originally founded in 1917 to help people coming home with serious injuries from the First World War.

Today it is the only outpatient rehabilitation center in the New York City area. ICD is dedicated to helping disabled individuals utilize their skills and attributes to the fullest as self-sufficient individuals. They help people with a vast range of problems from chemical dependency to brain injuries. Volunteer opportunities include vocational training, assisting with therapy, tutoring, filing, bookkeeping, and working in the library. Generally, opportunities are during weekdays. Interview, orientation, medical exam (provided).

THE JEWISH GUILD FOR THE BLIND
15 W. 66th St.
New York, NY 10023
Contact: Lyn Stone, Director of Volunteer Services
(212) 769-6217

Founded in 1914, the guild not only serves thousands of blind and visually impaired individuals every day, but also serves the multiply handicapped and others who suffer from various illnesses. The guild's 300 + volunteers work as classroom assistants, help serve meals, work as recreational assistants, lead field trips, write letters, help blind people pay their bills, head discussion groups, read newspaper articles for broadcast, record best-selling books for the Guild's 1,400 + -title cassette library, and serve as escorts for outings ranging from field and pleasure trips to medical appointments. Entertainers including singers, musicians, and comics are also encouraged to volunteer their time. Interview and orientation.

THE LIGHTHOUSE
111 E. 59th St.
New York, NY 10022
Contact: Carol Robbins, Director of Volunteer Services
(212) 821-9405

Now almost 100 years old, the Lighthouse, the nation's leading vision rehabilitation agency, uses volunteers to provide reading services to adults who are vision-impaired. Volunteers work on a one-to-one basis in regular day and evening sessions. The Lighthouse also runs a store called the Spectrum, which sells merchandise made for use by the visually impaired consumer. Volunteers are utilized as salespersons and information specialists. Every spring, the Lighthouse holds a three-day "POSH Sale" of high-quality clothing, new and previously worn. Over 100 volunteers with stamina are needed to stay on their feet and sell.

There is a training program to familiarize volunteers with the Lighthouse and its functions. Telephone customer service work is also available, especially for those who'd like to volunteer in the evenings. Interview.

NATIONAL DOWN SYNDROME SOCIETY
666 Broadway
Eighth Floor
New York, NY 10012
Contact: Myra Madnick, Executive Director
(212) 460-9330 or (800) 221-4602

Founded in 1979, NDSS is a national organization that serves families of persons with Down syndrome, providing assistance and information. NDSS is dedicated to creating and carrying out programs that (1) enable people with Down syndrome to achieve their fullest potential and (2) help science improve the health of people today and find answers for tomorrow. NDSS programs include Project Child, which enables a child with Down Syndrome to visit and share experiences with a volunteer family, an advocacy program, a clinical care program, a program for the aging, and more. Volunteers can assist in fund-raising events; graphic designers are welcome, as are library volunteers. Interview, orientation.

RECORDING FOR THE BLIND
545 Fifth Ave.
New York, NY 10017
Contact: Myra Shein, Studio Director
(212) 557-5720

If you'd like to help visually impaired people appreciate a wide range of literature, this is a wonderful opportunity.

Knowledgeable volunteers (you must have a college background) work with readers (also volunteers, who have passed a proficiency test) on educational material in various subjects including math, chemistry, law, and history. Monitors edit and produce recordings, operate tape recorders, make corrections in phrasing and pronunciation, maintain good sound quality, and so on. A minimum commitment of two hours a week is necessary. You can choose days, evenings, or even Saturdays. The finished recordings are available for the visually impaired or learning disabled five and older. Interview, training.

THE SALVATION ARMY
4133 Park Ave.
Bronx, NY 10457
Contact: Captain Lynn Gensler
(718) 583-3500
The Salvation Army's Adult Rehabilitation Center provides a residential program for men with treatable handicaps and for alcoholics. There is an ongoing need for individuals who wish to teach classes in math, arts and crafts, reading, interview techniques for jobs, writing a résumé, and so on. Classes are taught primarily on weekends and weekday evenings. Interview.

13

Miscellaneous

A brief potpourri of other important volunteer opportunities.

BETTER BUSINESS BUREAU
257 Park Ave. South
New York, NY 10010
Contact: Melissa Mann, Volunteer Coordinator
(212) 533-7500
If you've been in a situation where you felt you were treated unfairly, you might want to help with consumer rights. You can work on the consumer public phone lines as a trained consumer adviser or in the area of mediation, handling cases arising from consumer complaints. You need no specific credentials; volunteers come from a wide variety of backgrounds. Clerical help and volunteers for special projects are also needed. The BBB requests that volunteers give six hours a week. Interview, references, training.

NEW YORK ASSOCIATION FOR NEW AMERICANS
17 Battery Place
New York, NY 10004-1102
Contact: JoAnn Goldberg
(212) 425-5051

Since 1949 NYANA has been helping refugees and immigrants settle in and acclimate to America. Their goal is to
assist these newcomers in becoming self-reliant, culturally in-
tegrated members of society. Projects include the NICE program (NYANA's Informal Conservations in English) and RAP
(the Russian Acculturation Program), which matches volunteers with recently arrived Russian refugees to lead discussion
groups on a wide range of topics. Other programs include
job-skills training and cultural sojourns. All use volunteers.
Interviews, training.

NEW YORK CITY AUXILIARY POLICE
120-55 Queens Blvd.
Kew Gardens, NY 11424
Contact: Auxiliary Coordinator at your local precinct
Main Number: (718) 520-9243

Want a badge with your name on it?

Nearly 4,000 strong, New York City's Auxiliary Police
might provide the exciting opportunity you're looking for.
The force places uniformed patrol officers in residential and
commercial areas at special events such as parades, mara-
thons, block parties, and street fairs. You can patrol malls and
shopping centers, help at houses of worship and school and
church crossings, and observe and report dangerous street
conditions. The minimum commitment is eight hours a
month or 126 hours a year. There is an extensive training
program, which includes police science, social science/crimi-
nal law, radio communications, and more. The 16-week
course is available in the evenings for nine-to-fivers.

SPENCE-CHAPIN SERVICES TO FAMILIES AND CHILDREN
6 E. 94th St.
New York, NY 10028
Contact: Arlene Brown, Director of Development
(212) 369-0300

One of New York's most prominent adoption agencies, Spence-Chapin considers volunteers to be "valuable unpaid staff."

At its thrift shop (1430 Third Avenue), presently open six days a week, the agency uses volunteers in sales and in the marking room, where they price items. The agency itself utilizes volunteers primarily for office work, in the development and communications departments, and in research and public relations. Interview, training.

Miscellaneous

VICTIMS FOR VICTIMS
119 W. 57th St.
New York, NY 10019
Contact: Volunteer Coordinator
(212) 431-1200

If you've been the victim of a crime, you can both receive and provide emotional assistance.

Victims for Victims assists the emotional recovery of victims of violent crime. For over 10 years, victims have supported other victims by exchanging ideas, meeting in discussion groups, and lending support in various ways. There are support groups, a companion program, and other opportunities for you to help. If you have been a crime victim, you can benefit others in similar situations. Interview.

WOMEN'S ACTION ALLIANCE
370 Lexington Avenue
Suite 603
New York, NY 10017
Contact: Tanya Nieri, Assistant to the Executive Director
(212) 523-8330, ext. 110

If you are interested in women's issues, you might check out the Women's Action Alliance. A national service organization, WAA works through community-based institutions to provide educational training and technical assistance to women's service providers and their clients. You can help in the information and referral service, in fund-raising, with special events, or with research. WAA also welcomes professionals: graphic designers, accountants, and so on. Résumé, interview, orientation, training.

14

Umbrella Organizations and Referral Groups

In this day of one-stop shopping, you can find volunteer opportunities through "umbrella groups" and referral services that specialize in finding a location that meets your interests, needs, and availability. These agencies will generally give you referrals and not simply try to place you in a position. Thus you have the flexibility to decide whether they've made a solid match.

Most of the groups listed below publish a significant amount of literature, sometimes including books of listings. National organizations, such as AmeriCorps, also have listings of volunteer work available in the city. (For AmeriCorps, call the Albany Office of Budget and Management at [518] 473-8882 to find out about opportunities in New York City.)

These services have listings and contacts throughout the five boroughs. They cover weekly posts and onetime special events, and they are designed, like this book, to save you the legwork and trouble of scouting possible volunteer alternatives.

Listings

FEDERATION OF PROTESTANT AND WELFARE AGENCIES
281 Park Ave. South
New York, NY 10010
Contact: Volunteer Services Department
(212) 777-4800
A self-described volunteer clearinghouse, this is among the leading referral centers in New York.

The federation refers volunteers to over 260 affiliated Protestant and nonsectarian social service and health-related agencies in all five boroughs and Long Island. All types of volunteers are utilized, including those who want to become board members of organizations, professionals who want to work on a pro bono basis, and the many who want to help homeless people, the elderly, children, HIV/AIDS patients, and more. The federation asks for at least two hours a week. Interview.

F.E.G.S.
62 W. 14th St.
Seventh Floor
New York, NY 10011
Contact: Volunteer and Internship Program
(212) 366-8144
For over 60 years, F.E.G.S. (Federation Employment and Guidance Service) has operated a network of social, vocational, and health-related services in Brooklyn, the Bronx,

Queens, Manhattan, and Long Island. This multipurpose agency has programs in the areas of addictions, HIV/AIDS, family violence, corporate services, home care, immigrant and refugee services, legal services, housing, vocational services, and much more. The volunteer program can help match your area of interest with one of those. Interview.

HISPANIC FEDERATION OF NEW YORK CITY
545 Eighth Ave.
11th Floor
New York, NY 10018
Contact: Diana Valentin, Volunteer Recruitment Program Coordinator
(212) 967-5407

The federation is designed to help social agencies better meet the needs of the Hispanic community. It recruits professionals to serve on boards of member agencies, and nonprofessionals to work on the day-to-day operations of the agencies. There are 56 organizations involved in the network, looking for volunteers to help mentor youths, raise funds, assist with administrative duties, and more. An orientation for newcomers is held every two to three months.

JEWISH BOARD OF FAMILY AND CHILDREN'S SERVICES
Mary S. Froelich Division of Volunteer Services
120 W. 57th St.
New York, NY 10019
Contact: Volunteer Division
(212) 397-4090

One of the largest agencies in the city, JBFCS is devoted to meeting the needs of people in crisis with compassion and meaningful care. As a volunteer you can become involved at one of over 70 locations, dealing with HIV/AIDS, family crises, day treatment services, case management, social services, immigrant and refugee services, and helping the learning-disabled. There are various outreach programs, and much more. Volunteers are trained and supervised to support therapeutic services in all five boroughs. Interview, references, training.

THE JEWISH COMMUNITY CENTER ON THE UPPER WEST SIDE
180 W. 80th St.
New York, NY 10024
Contact: Susan Zuckerman, Associate Director
(212) 580-0099

An important part of the JCC's role in the community is referring volunteers to agencies around New York City.

The JCC looks to meet the ever-changing needs of the community with social, cultural, and educational programs. From preschool programs to after-school recreational activities, the center offers various opportunities for neighborhood youngsters. There are also activities and groups for adults, including single parents and seniors. Volunteers are matched with the program that suits their interests: Sukkah decorating at local hospitals, helping the Jewish Teen Theater group, or working with new readers in the Gift of Literacy program. Interview.

See also chapter 7, "Community."

MAYOR'S VOLUNTARY ACTION CENTER
61 Chambers St.
New York, NY 10007
Contact: Just tell them you'd like to volunteer.
(212) 788-7550

Placing people like you in volunteer positions since 1967, MVAC works with nearly 5,000 volunteer agencies, corporations, and educational institutions throughout the city, referring volunteers to a variety of positions. Opportunities are abundant in the areas of health, recreation, education, human services, and culture. In addition, MVAC has numerous special programs, including the Clothing Bank, which provides new clothes to more than 450 agencies and shelters serving the city's homeless. There is also the innovative Family Matters program, designed to find opportunities for families to volunteer together in their community. Additionally, MVAC provides workshops and training events, as well as task forces which include student volunteer programs, HIV/AIDS programs and more. In recognition of a job well done they also issue the annual Mayor's Volunteer Service Awards. Interview.

Umbrella Organizations . . .

NEW YORK CARES
116 E. 16th St.
New York, NY 10003-2112
Contact: Just tell them you want to volunteer.
(212) 228-5000

Twenty-five hundred volunteers per month in 150 programs can't be wrong. You can become one such volunteer, involved in either long-term or short-term projects, through New York Cares. Opportunities range from tutoring a student through the school year to a one-day city cleanup project. Looking to meet the needs of the full-time working community, New York Cares has numerous opportunities on weekends and before or after regular working hours. Interested volunteers receive a menu of activities, flexible schedules, and various commitment options. Among NYC's ongoing signature projects are the Coat Drive and New York Cares Day, when thousands of volunteers are mobilized for a one-day marathon of community service. Other opportunities include hospital support; tutoring; outreach programs; public school programs; and work with the elderly, homeless and disadvantaged people, and HIV/AIDS patients. Interview, orientation.

ST. VINCENT DE PAUL SOCIETY
1011 First Ave.
New York, NY 10022
Contact: Luke Finn, Program Director
(212) 755-8615

A grassroots organization founded in France in the mid-1800s, the society has chapters throughout the world. For a century and a half it has provided charitable services to the poor, the suffering, and the needy through family help, food distribution, prison visitation, clothing distribution, working with youth, and the burial of indigents. Utilizing 16 church locations throughout the city, the society provides nearly $9,000 worth of food a month for the homeless and otherwise unfortunate. It also has a summer camp program for 450 children aged 6–12. Staffed primarily by volunteers, the camp program is a great way for college students to get involved. Interview, orientation.

UNITED HOSPITAL FUND
350 Fifth Avenue
23rd Floor
New York, NY 10118
Contact: Volunteer Hot Line
(212) 675-6644
**To volunteer at the United Hospital Fund itself, contact Susan Wyant,
(212) 494-0700**

The United Hospital Fund is an umbrella agency for New York City hospitals that matches prospective volunteers with a hospital in their neighborhood. The UHF will try to determine what you would like to do and find you the opportunity. There are positions working with patients or in other areas of a hospital. You can even become involved in the UHF itself by joining its committee on health care legislation or its City Hospital Visiting Committee, which monitors patient care and staff conditions. Call the hot line, leave a message, and receive their volunteer package. Interview.

See also chapter 12, "Health and Human Services."

UNITED JEWISH APPEAL–FEDERATION OF NEW YORK
130 E. 59th St.
New York, NY 10022
Contact: Sally Pearce, Volunteer Coordinator
(212) 753-2288

The UJA–Federation network of agencies helps over 4.5 million people a year, "one at a time," in New York, Israel, and worldwide. The federation works in conjunction with Y's, community centers, counseling centers, hospitals, and a wide variety of nearly 100 agencies throughout all five boroughs. Volunteers can help in health, education, community matters, professional counseling, and recreational activities; they can advocate for and work toward enhancing the Jewish community worldwide. You can also assist the UJA–Federation itself at community-wide events. Interview.

Umbrella Organizations . . .

UNITED WAY OF NEW YORK CITY
99 Park Ave.
New York, NY 10016
Contact: Volunteers in Action
(212) 973-3922

The United Way represents a tremendous number of health and human services agencies throughout the city. There are a number of programs that will match your skills with a program and opportunity that are right for you—working in a hospital or soup kitchen, helping the homeless, mentoring youngsters, assisting the elderly, working in community centers and settlement houses, or any of numerous other possibilities. Besides the Volunteers in Action program for individual volunteers, the United Way has a "Corporate Volunteer Program" that might appeal to your office or company. Call for a directory.

VOLUNTEER REFERRAL SERVICE
161 Madison Ave.
New York, NY 10016
Contact: Just ask for an appointment.
(212) 745-8249 for appointment; (212) 889-4805 office

The Volunteer Referral Service interviews potential volunteers to help them determine what they'd like to do, and then helps them find several such opportunities. The VRS looks for a commitment of at least two hours a week for the many affiliated agencies (mostly in Manhattan). The VRS's offerings include all kinds of volunteer opportunities. Both day and evening interviews are available.

YORKVILLE CIVIC COUNCIL
48 E. 92nd St.
New York, NY 10128
Contact: Council Office
(212) 427-5629

Founded in the late 1920s, this nonprofit membership organization comprises the leaders of nearly 160 community organizations including civic, cultural, educational, health, religious, and social groups. There are individual members, too. The council serves Manhattan's Upper East Side and has a well-researched brochure that lists over 100 neighborhood locations, from hospitals to museums to halfway houses, that can use your help. It is also a source for information on volunteering in this busy community. For the brochure, send a self-addressed, stamped envelope to the Yorkville Civic Council at the above address.

Umbrella Organizations . . .

A Few Parting Words . . .

Volunteering is a special part of life. Believe me, I know. There is no monetary equal to the joy and appreciation displayed by the smiling faces of those people you have helped. We hope that we've pointed you in the right direction with our listings and information about volunteering, and that now you're ready to go out and make a difference.

Think about the area that suits you best; make the time, make the calls, go for the interviews, and become one of the millions of people who enjoy this wonderful side of life.

My parents taught me by example, and I hope to show my children the warmth and good feelings that come from doing for others. If you've been there, you know what I'm talking about, and if you haven't, let me assure you that volunteering can give you a feeling of gratification and accomplishment you won't get anyplace else.

Try it. You'll be glad you did.

Subject Index

Subject Index

Index of
Organizations by
Borough

Index of Organizations

Index of Organizations